THE AUTOBIOGRAPHY

OF

THE EMPEROR CHARLES V.

RECENTLY DISCOVERED IN THE PORTUGUESE
LANGUAGE BY BARON KERVYN DE LETTENHOVE, MEMBER
OF THE ROYAL ACADEMY OF BELGIUM.

THE ENGLISH TRANSLATION BY

LEONARD FRANCIS SIMPSON,

M.R.S.L.

COPYRIGHT EDITION.

LONDON:

LONGMAN, GREEN, LONGMAN, ROBERTS, & GREEN.

1862.

THE

AUTOBIOGRAPHY OF CHARLES V.

OR

SUMMARY OF THE VOYAGES AND EXPEDITIONS UNDER-
TAKEN BY THE EMPEROR CHARLES V. SINCE HIS
DEPARTURE FROM THE STATES OF FLANDERS (WHERE
HE WAS BORN ON FEBRUARY 24, 1500, ACCORDING TO
ROMAN STYLE, AND WHERE HE WAS EDUCATED),
AFTER THE DEATH OF KING PHILIP HIS FATHER,
WHOM GOD HAVE IN HIS GLORY! WHICH HAPPENED
IN THE YEAR 1516.

CONTENTS.

CHAPTER III.

CHAPTER IV.

CHAPTER V.

CHAPTER IX.

CHAPTER X.

INTRODUCTION

BY

BARON KERVYN DE LETTENHOVE.

———◦✦◦———

FOR some years the attention of the most eminent minds has been earnestly directed to the study of the history of the sixteenth century, and Charles V., who occupies the first place in that history, is indebted to a greater impartiality, as well as to the revelations of a great number of unpublished documents, for a tardy justice to his memory. Where it had been agreed to accuse him of ambition, sincere convictions have been recognised, which neither numerous obstacles nor long sufferings could alter; and his abdication itself, by showing him superior to all the grandeurs he had traversed, has shed a calm and serene halo upon the last years of his life, of which there are few examples in the agitated career of the rulers of the world.

In our days, it is no longer the case that historiographers alone and official _coronistes_ are consulted; men study especially those intimate narrators who, without burnishing their narrative by a pomp which always excites some mistrust, adhere strictly to truth. At times it is necessary to refer to the confidential reports of the skillful negotiators of Venice to judge the Emperor at the apogee of his power; again, to follow him in the repose which he sought in the shade of a cloister, we must interrogate the remembrances of those Hieronymite monks who saw him day by day bending towards the tomb where their prayers were to follow him. The same interest is attached to the familiar letters written by his most faithful servants, and among those there are none more valuable than the letters addressed to Louis de Praet by William van Male, who close to his person had admired the glory of the Emperor before climbing with him that rough pass of Puerto-Novo, when Charles V. exclaimed, ' This is the last pass that I shall have to cross before that of death!'

William van Male was born at Bruges. His

family does not appear to have belonged to
the ancient noblesse, and he was poorly provided with the gifts of fortune. For a long
time his sole occupation had been to shut
himself up in his library, which he afterwards
called 'the dear prison of his youth.' Finally,
he found himself reduced to seek his fortune
in Spain, and attached himself to the Duke
of Alba, who was then only the generous and
brilliant Captain, who was called 'the father
of the soldiers;' through him he was enabled
to gain admission to the cabinet of the Emperor, not to solicit the honour of girding on
a sword, but to consult a manuscript relating
to the war in Germany, by Don Louis d'Avila,
much more complete than that which had been
published in Spanish in 1548. William van
Male managed so well that he was allowed to
translate it into Latin, and, thanks to the re-
commendation either of the Duke of Alba,*
or of Louis d'Avila himself, Cosmo de Medici
— the great Cosmo, as Brantôme calls him —
accepted the dedication of that work, which

* Cosmo de Medici had married a cousin of the Duke of
Alba, Eleanor of Toledo.

narrated in a pure and elegant style the events
which had recently taken place.

On the conclusion of a dedicatory epistle to
the Duke of Florence, William van Male
expresses himself as follows : —

If it is thought that I do not reply completely
enough to the reproaches which might be addressed
to me, people must at least bow before the sound
judgement and high intellect of the illustrious Seigneur de Praet. The latter, always animated by an
admirable zeal for learned men, has kindly consented
to read this book before it was published, and passed
the file of his enlightened mind over those parts
which appeared to him rough and unpolished.*

It will be readily understood that William
van Male attached much value to the approval
of Seigneur de Praet, who was a Knight of the
Golden Fleece, at the head of the Finances of

---

* Qua ratione, si obtrectatoribus per me non factum est satis,
vereantur sanè necesse est Illustriss. D. Pratensis acerrimum
judicium et gravitatem. Is enim pro incredibili quadam erga
studiosos omnes humanitate, libellum prius quam ederetur,
diligenter perlegit, quæque inexpolita et rudia viderentur, iis
perspicacissimi ingenii sui limam addidit. Ipse itaque celsitu-
dinem tuam in partem defensionis juvabit, si vitilitigatorum
tædio et molestia affectus, eos ad tantam Principis viri dignita-
tem et eruditionem relegaveris.

the Netherlands, and who, moreover, held the office of Grand Bailiff of Bruges.*

To this testimony of the honourable relations of the translator of Louis d'Avila's work, a few lines must be added, in which he proclaims the mission incumbent upon letters of perpetuating the glory of the Emperor, and wherein he insists upon the legitimate authority of the historian, when it has been his lot to take a striking part in the exploits narrated in his recital.

* Louis de Flandre, Seigneur de Praet, descended from Louis de Male, last Count of Flanders. His mother, Isabella of Burgundy, was, also in illegitimate line, the great-grand-daughter of Philip the Good; her grandmother, Louise de la Gruthruse, was the sister of that illustrious Seigneur de la Gruthruse, who was not less honoured by the hospitality he gave to King Edward at York than by the protection he accorded to letters by having MSS. copied and enriched with sumptuous miniatures. Louis de Praet shared the same tastes. Xenophon, Plato, Polybius, Cicero, Seneca, were his favourite authors: he corresponded with Vivès and Viglius, and the historian of the Counts of Flanders, Jacques Meyerus, addressed an ode to him, in which he says —

'All the Muses bear thee up towards heaven. The historians who relate thy great deeds, and the poets that sing them, call you their father and their Mecænas. You are our glory and the honour of our country, you who count among your ancestors the kings and princes whom Flanders has obeyed. How can I praise you sufficiently? The nobility of thy origin is heightened by so many virtues, it is revealed to the world by so many brilliant acts, that even should old Homer, the bard of the kings of Greece, return among us, his lays would not suffice for thy glory.'

It is probable that William van Male returned to Brussels with the Duke of Alba and the son of Charles V. Van Male, who aspired to write the contemporary annals of the Netherlands, doubtless did not foresee the future when he saw that young prince, who was afterwards Philip II., preside at a festival between the Duke of Alba and the Counts of Egmont and of Hornes, in that great square at Brussels, where afterwards . . . . . But then his country presented itself only to the heart of Van Male surrounded by images of prosperity and of happiness,* and he entreated Louis de Praet to find for him some honourable position, which might lead to his appointment as Belgian historiographer of the Emperor.

It was about the Easter festivities of 1550 that Louis de Praet obtained for William van Male the situation of *Ayuda de Cámara* in the Emperor's household, and Charles V., who was fond of literature, and regretted that he had not cultivated letters sufficiently during his youth, took him at once into his intimacy. Did

---

* Malinæum tuum plane beaveris. — *Lettres de Guillaume van Male*, published by M. de Reiffenberg, p. 10.

Charles V. confine himself to repeat to William van Male certain recitals which he had borrowed from Louis d'Avila? Did he ask him to explain to him, according to the Latin text, the commentaries of Cæsar, which he only knew from a translation in the tongue of Dante and of Macchiavelli? It is only allowed to suppose so: but what we know with more certainty is, that the Emperor honoured him daily with long interviews, that Van Male was incessantly occupied reading or writing under his dictation near his table or at the fireside, even at night at his bedside,* and that he was, in some measure, as he himself expresses it, tied to a post by his functions and occupations.†

On May 31, 1550, Charles V. left Brussels for Germany on important business. On reaching Cologne he embarked on June 14 on the Rhine, and took five days to reach Mayence. William van Male, who accompanied the Emperor, hastened to write to Mayence to his

---

* Quotidianum colloquium . . . ad forum. In lectione nocturna . . . — *Lettres de Guillaume van Male,* pp. 26, 27, 35, 45.

† Tanquam ad palum alligatus. — *Ibid.,* p. 54.

illustrious friend, Louis de Praet; but this letter, the loss of which cannot be too much regretted, no longer exists, and we only know its contents * from a rapid recapitulation † which Van Male inserted in another letter, also addressed to Seigneur de Praet, and written at Augsburg on July 17, 1550. We reproduce it here, borrowing the faithful translation of it, published by M. Mignet:—

In the leisures of his navigation on the Rhine, the Emperor, having plenty of leisure time on board ship, undertook to write his journeys and expeditions from the year 1515 up to the present moment. The work is admirably polished and elegant, and the style attests great strength of mind and eloquence. Surely, I should not easily have imagined that the Emperor possessed such qualifications, as he has avowed to me himself that he was indebted for nothing to education, and that he had acquired them entirely by his own meditations and labour. As regards the weight and value of the work, they consist especially

* Intelligo nullas e meis [litteris] tibi redditas esse . . . Scripseram fusissime . . . Despero hujus infortunii memor quod litteræ meæ sint interceptæ.—*Lettres de Guillaume* van *Male*, pp. 11, 12.

† Brevem anacephaleosim. *Ibid*, p. 12.

in that fidelity and that gravity to which history owes its credit and its power.*

William van Male added in a postscript : —

The Emperor has allowed me to translate his work as soon as it has been revised by Granvelle and by his son. I have resolved to adopt a new style, which partakes at the same time of Titus Livius, of Cæsar, of Suetonius, and of Tacitus; but the Emperor is unjust towards us and our century when he wishes his work to remain secret, and protected by a hundred keys.†

If anyone is desirous of knowing what William van Male meant by this new system of

---

* Scripsi e Mogunciaco Cæsaris iter; liberalissimas ejus occupationes in navigatione fluminis Rheni, dum otii occasione invitatus, scriberet in navi peregrinationes suas et expeditiones, quas ab anno XV. in præsentem usque diem suscepisset . . . Libellus est mire tersus et elegans, utpote magna ingenii et eloquentiæ vi conscriptus. Ego certe non temere credidissem Cæsari illas quoque dotes inesse, quum, ut ipse mihi fatetur, nihil talium rerum institutione sit consecutus, sed sola meditatione et cura. Quod attinet ad auctoramentum et gratiam, vide, obsecro, quibus fulcris innitentur, scilicet fide et dignitate, quibus potissimum duobus et commendatur et viget historia.

† Cæsar indulsit mihi libri sui versionem, ubi fuerit per Granvellanum et filium recognitas. Statui novum quoddam scribendi temperamentum effingere, mixtum et Livio, Cæsare, Suetonio, et Tacito. Iniquus est tamen Cæsar nobis et sæculo, quod rem supprimi velit et servari centum clavibus. — *Lettres da Guillaume van Male*, p. 13.

interpretation, he may refer to what he himself
wrote on the subject of the narrative of Don
Louis d'Avila : —

It is right that deeds which have surpassed what
has been most famous in divers countries should be
narrated in a celebrated language, and understood
by all nations. Perhaps I may be accused of employing a new and too free system of translation;
I have followed the exact text before me, without,
however, holding myself bound to give it literally,
but without altering the sense, even when I have
not adopted the same order and the same words.

The conqueror of Barbarossa, like the conqueror of Gaul, had endeavoured, to quote an
expression of Montaigne, to recommend, not his
sayings, but his acts.* Van Male wished this
book to offer, at the same, time, a model to warriors and to historians; † his idea, therefore, was
to give to the Commentaries of the Emperor a
classical tinge of Latin literature to bring the
ancient and the new Cæsar into approximation.

---

* Si les gestes de Xénophon et de César n'eussent de bien
loing surpassé leur éloquence, je ne croy pas qu'ils les eussent
jamais escripts; ils ont cherché à recommander non leur dire,
mais leur faire. — *Essais*, i. 39.

† Les commentaires de César, dit Plutarque, ont été loués
par les meilleurs esprits de son temps, comme un modèle par-
fait de ce genre d'ouvrage, et comme également propres à
former les historiens et les guerriers.

At Augsburg Charles V. closeted himself
with Van Male to dictate to him, four hours
consecutively. It was here that he complèted
the work which extended from 1516 to the
month of September 1548. Did the Emperor,
in terminating his recitals at the end of the year
1548, consider them as given summarily in the
most clear and precise form in the instructions
which he transmitted to his son on January 18
of that same year? * There also he dwelt upon
the infirmities which tormented him, the dangers
which he had braved, the uncertainty of God's
intentions towards him, before tracing the rules
which his successor would later have to adopt in
his policy. First, it was an absolute devotion to
religion, which, without weakness as without
usurpation, should maintain the hopes attached
to the convocation of the Council of Trent:
abroad it was a prudent and skillful system,
which should not compromise the relations with
France, and should seek the friendship of England; at home a generous and conciliating

---

* Sandoval (édition d'Anvers), ii. p. 475—*Papiers d'État de
Granvelle*, iii. 267. I have seen an Italian translation of these
instructions in the Vatican Library, No. 756.

government in Germany, active and vigilant in
Italy, wise and enlightened in the Netherlands,
which had always shown themselves hostile to
foreign rule; * finally, he recommended to him,
everywhere and always, the love of peace, which
the very experience of wars ought to render
more intense, economy in the administration of
the finances, impartiality in that of justice, sup-
pression of abuses, respect for the rights of all
men.   In these instructions, as in his Commentaries, Charles V. had incessantly before his eyes
the instability of human things.†

William van Male assures us, moreover, that
Charles V. wished to continue his Commentaries up to the last moment.‡   Doubtless he
could not find time, and the dictations which
have been preserved to us occupied in 1550
and in 1551 the greater portion of the leisure
hours he had at his disposal at Augsburg, under
the refreshing shade of the Fugger Gardens.§

---

* Los de alli no pueden bien suffrir ser governados por
estrangeros.
† La continua instabilidad y mudança de las cossas ter-
renas.
‡ In præsentem usque diem. — *Lettres de Guillaume van
Male*, p. 12.
§ I dare not say all those leisure hours, as I find from a

Did the Emperor carry out the more or less vague promise which he made at Mayence? Did he commence submitting his work to the revision of his son, then in his twenty-third year, and to that of Granvelle? The negative seems but little doubtful, for nothing has been found in connection with such a communication. The last lines of the *postscriptum* of the letter of July 17, already announced, as M. Mignet shrewdly observes, that the Emperor had altered his intention, and on reading the later letters of Van Male, we only find him somewhat laboriously occupied with the publication, which the Emperor had imposed upon him, of his translation of the 'Chevalier délibéré' of Olivier de la Marche. It seemed that Charles V., on the point of touching upon the most difficult period of his life, endeavoured to draw himself away from modern history, troubled, agitated, disturbed, replete with struggles, harassed by hesitation and doubts, to find recreation in the

note for which I am indebted to the kindness of our learned perpetual secretary, M. Quetelet, that Hulsius mentions a treatise which Charles V., about the same time, is said to have composed on artillery; viz. 'Discorso de l'artilleria de l'imperadore Carlo V., scritto a mano, 1552.'

fables of chivalry, which itself was already nothing more than a poetical fiction.

Nevertheless, at the end of the year 1551, Charles V. took up his residence at Inspruck, where he was nearer to Italy; but he soon regretted having done so. The distance he was at from the centre of Germany encouraged the efforts of his enemies, and the absence of any army which might have protected him made him in some measure a prey to their audacity.

On April 4, 1552, Charles V. wrote thus to his brother, the King of the Romans :—

I find myself actually without power or authority. I find myself obliged to abandon Germany, not having anyone to support me there, and so many opponents, and already the power in their hands. What a fine end I shall have for my old age! . . . Everything well considered, recommending myself to God, and placing myself in His hands; seeing at this hour the necessity of submitting either to great shame or of placing myself in a great danger. I prefer taking the part of the danger, as it is in the hand of God to remedy it, than to await that of shame, which is so apparent.*

* Lanz. Corresp. des Kaisers Karl V., iii. p. 161. Bucholz, Geschichte der Regierung Ferdinand des Ersten, ix. p. 549.

The following is the text of the Emperor's letter : —

Je me trouve présentement desnué de forces et desauctorisé. Je me vois forcé d'abandonner l'Alle-mayne pour n'avoir nul qui se veuille déclarer pour moy, et tant de contraires, et jà les forces en leurs mains. . . . Quelle bel fin je feroie en mes vieulx jours ! . . . Le tout bien considéré, me recom-mandant à Dieu et me mettant en ses mains, voyant à cette heure nécessité de recevoir une grande honte ou de me mettre en ung grand danger, j'ayme mieulx prendre la part du danger, puisqu'il est en la main de Dieu de le remédier, que attendre celle de la honte, qui est si apparente.

Six weeks afterwards, Charles V. was com-pelled precipitately to leave Inspruck during the night, not to fall into the hands of his enemies.

Under these grave circumstances, Charles V., threatened in his authority and in his liberty, was concerned about the fate reserved to his memoirs, in which he had explained the secrets of his policy, and judged the faults of the Pro-testant princes of Germany. He thought it prudent to intrust them to some devoted ser-vant, who could take them to Spain beyond all danger, and he added a few lines addressed to his son, in which he revealed to him the importance of this deposit, which was not to be opened until at an epoch or on an eventuality which he meant to indicate. In the midst of the alarms and emotions of Inspruck those lines remained incomplete; but, despite the French and Turkish galleys which were cruising in the Mediterranean, the mission was faithfully executed, and the narrative dictated by Charles V. to Van Male was remitted (everything at least announces it) to the young Prince of Spain.

As soon as the troops of Maurice of Saxony had entered Inspruck, they pillaged everything which had belonged to the Emperor. His books and papers, which were in Van Male's house, shared the same fate. Were the Protestants aware, from the letter Van Male wrote at Mayence, which was intercepted, as he relates, of the existence of the imperial work? It would doubtless have been the most precious part of the booty which they made.

Between the flight from Inspruck, which aroused the indignation of Don Juan of Austria, and the abdication of Brussels, so easily accepted by Philip II., there was no time for the continuation of the Commentaries: each day had its combats and its dangers, or at least its struggles, of every description, and its renewed agitations. But what happened later at Yuste? Opinions are divided: we shall endeavour to explain our own.

Charles V. had the fixed intention of completing in silence and in peace the work which he had commenced in the midst of wars and of political struggles. He wished to show, by justifying his conduct towards popes and kings, that in the religious troubles of Germany, as in the great wars against France, he always remained what he had been on the burning shores of Tunis and of Algeria—the real chief and legitimate representative of the Christian polity, which was violently threatened at home as well as abroad.* He hoped, he said in a letter, every sentence of which we shall have carefully to consider, to do something

---

* 'The Emperor,' writes Tiepolo, 'neglects nothing of what we have a right to expect from a Christian Emperor full of zeal for faith and for the Church.' (See *Chronique de Charles-Quint,* par M. Pichot, p. 149.)

which God should not judge useless to His service.

He took with him into his retreat his able Secretary, William van Male, and, declaring that he had resolved no longer to occupy himself with the affairs of the present, he had announced immediately on his arrival in Spain, that he intended sending away all his attendants, with the exception of Van Male,* that is to say, to be able to shut himself up with him as he did at Augsburg, and the better shielded against all ideas of vanity, as these memoirs of his life would be traced at the foot of his tomb.

However, other occupations came to interrupt these plans, and Van Male, who became such a favourite that he excited all the jealousy of the Spaniards, seemed to have shared his days in reading to the Emperor during his dinner, and in drawing up bulletins relative to his health, which were addressed regularly to the Secretary of State, Don Juan Vasquez.†

* Lettre de Gastelù, du 11 Oct., 1556.—*Retraite et Mort de Charles-Quint*, par M. Gachard, i. pp. 18 and 19.

† Lettre de Guillaume van Male, du 11 Avril, 1557.— Gachard, *Retraite et Mort de Charles-Quint*, ii. p. 167.

There were two distinct periods in the sojourn of Charles V. at Yuste (St. Just). During the first, still dreaming of the restoration of his strength and health, which had been prematurely weakened, he wished to create for himself in his solitude, less sombre than it was at a later period, commodious buildings, gardens planted with lemon and orange-trees, sparkling fountains and basins full of trout. In the second, struggling in vain against the malady which ravaged his body without affecting the vigour of his intellect, he beheld only in the remembrances of his glory his weaknesses and his miseries, and his mind, absorbed by pious meditations, detached itself from earthly things. Read through the letters (and they are very numerous) which were written at Yuste by the attendants of Charles V.; you will find therein all the incidents, all the episodes, of his daily life, but you will not find any trace of the historical dictations to William van Male; and if there may be a few allusions, far from recompensing on a large basis the apology of that most chequered life, they are reduced to broken fragments.

Charles V., it is true, was occupied at times with thinking what judgement posterity would pass upon him; but at those moments he recommended to be collected carefully the vast compilations of Florian Ocampo and of Ginés Sepulveda.* However, it so happened that he said to Father Francis de Borgia, whom he had charged with a mission to Portugal —

Do you think that there is any sign of vanity in writing one's own acts? You must know that I have related all the expeditions (*jornadas*) that I have undertaken, with the causes and motives which urged me to them, but I have not been actuated, in writing, by any desire of glory, or any idea of vanity.†

It is impossible for us not to see in these words of Charles V. an allusion to his work of 1550, which he had entitled 'Summario das Viages e Jornadas,' adding thereunto a letter protesting that he had not composed it out of vanity. It appears that Charles V., in forgetting

* Lettre de l'Empereur, du 9 Juillet, 1558. — Gachard, *Retraite et Mort de Charles-Quint*, i. p. 310.

† Ribadeneyra, *vida del P. Francisco de Borja*, p. 113.; Sandoval (éd. d'Anvers), ii. p. 617. Compare what Sepulveda says: 'that Charles V. saw a proof of ambition in the encouragement which certain princes granted to recitals which were favourable to them.'

at Yuste all his great and glorious acts, has given the strongest proof of humility, and the President of the Council of Castille, Juan de Vega, on hearing of his death, wrote —

No noise of his armies, with which he had often made the world tremble, had followed him to the monastery of Yuste; he had forgotten his steel-clad battalions and his floating banners as completely as if all the days of his life had been passed in that solitude.*

The testimony of Ambrosia de Moralès is still much more precise than that of Juan de Vega. Ambrosia de Moralès, who wrote in 1564, six years after the death of Charles V., affirms that his Commentaries were not composed at Yuste, but in Germany. ‘What (he says) ought espe-‘cially to excite admiration is that this Prince ‘himself, in the midst of the fury of his wars,† ‘drew up an exact and sequent narrative of his ‘acts.’

In the enumeration of the books found at Yuste after the death of Charles V. we find the

---

* Sandoval, *Vida del Emp. Carlos V. en Yuste* (éd. d’Anvers), p. 619.

† En toda la braveza de sus guerras.

following:—A book of memoirs (*Memorias*),with
a golden pen. Did this book of memoirs con-
tain the Commentaries? Was that golden pen
the Emperor's pen, left forgotten between two
unfinished pages? It must be observed that
Granvelle designates the Commentaries as *Mé-
moires,* and the place itself which this notice
occupies in the inventory, side by side with the
Emperor's papers, and the maps which he consulted, is of some importance. But how comes
it that the notary or clerk who, in describing the
cups and spoons, always points out what use
was made of them by the Emperor, could have
forgotten to add that those memoirs were neither
accounts nor notes (the word *Memorias* signifies
both), but the autobiography of Charles V.?

There were also at Yuste a portfolio of black
velvet and papers intrusted to the care of
William van Male. This doubtless contained
the political correspondence of Charles V., but
Quijada took from him at the same time, and
almost forcibly * (Van Male complained of it
bitterly), the sheets which contained the text of

---

* Quasi por fuerça, Lettre du Cardinal de Granvelle, du 7
Mars, 1561.—*Papiers d'Etat de Granvelle,* vi. p. 200.

the Commentaries, such as they had been written under the Emperor's dictation.

'That is my work!' exclaimed Van Male;[*] and here again it can only be question of an unfinished manuscript in many points, as Van Male assured us that the greater portion of it was engraven on his memory.[†]

What became of those manuscripts, complete or incomplete, left such as they issued from the first dictation, or partially revised and touched up? Did Philip II. destroy them? We dare not either accuse him of it or absolve him of it. Assuredly he would never have authorised their publication; but he allowed Moralès, his historiographer, to quote the memorable example of Charles V. writing his own history, and the very preservation of the manuscript sent from Inspruck is an irrefutable argument.[‡]

[*] Diziendo que eran sus travajos.—*Papiers d'Etat de Granvelle*, vi. p. 200.

[†] Tenia en la memoria buena parte.—*Ibid.*

[‡] Does the codicil of Philip II., which orders certain papers to be burnt after his death, refer to the Commentaries of Charles V? This appears to me very difficult of admission. Could Phillip II. have designated the work of his father by these terms, as vague as they are disdainful : 'Papeles de otras qualesquier personas especialmente de los defunctos'? and how is it compatible with that system of reserve which is applicable to

Did Van Male, who had returned to Spain laden with rewards, and who, moreover, had the distinguished honour of being mentioned in the will of Charles V., execute from gratitude* his project of taxing his memory for the elements of a new text of the Commentaries.† Did he

all important papers that are to be preserved : 'Papel de importancia que convenga guardar.'

* Por memoria.—*Papiers d'Etat du Cardinal de Granvelle,* vi. p. 290.

† M. Arendt fancies to have found in the long account of the capture of Hesdin and Térouanne, by Sepulveda, an extract from the Commentaries of Charles V., completed at Yuste. If those Commentaries had devoted sixteen long chapters to the capture of those two towns, what extent would it not be necessary to attribute to them? It appears only that Van Male had pictured to Sepulveda that campaign as of very great importance, and that he had promised him a detailed narrative of it. But there is not the slightest allusion to a source which would have been treated with the utmost respect. If Sepulveda had thought to attain from Van Male the communication of a fragment of the Commentaries of Charles V., would he not have solicited that of some other more important portion? It must also be observed that Sepulveda's letter was published in 1557. Now, of two things, one—either he would not have dared to mention the communication of Charles V., who was still alive, if he had prohibited it, or, had he authorised it, his generosity (*humanitatem*) would have been extolled. Charles V. was not present at those two sieges, and all that we know gives rise to the belief that he only related at any length those expeditions in which he took a direct and immediate part. It is, however, easily understood that Van Male could procure from his friends in Flanders some detailed narrative of an expedition of which they were witnesses. M. de

take advantage of his leisure hours in his native land to compose that Latin translation, which would at the same time have recalled the great actions of modern times and the most perfect literary works of the ancients? We are reduced to the testimony of Cardinal de Granvelle,* who relates that Van Male complained at not having been able to commence his work, because he had always been unwell, and suffering since his return. In fact, Van Male died on January 1, 1561, two years and three months after him whom he loved to call his master.†

Van Male, as we also learn from Cardinal de Granvelle, had many friends,‡ with whom he

Reiffenberg observes (Introduction to 'Van Male's Letters,' p. 20) that many well-informed persons had promised to provide him with reliable and circumstantial accounts. Macchetus, publishing in 1555 a narrative of that campaign, at which he was present, says that there exist others where the same facts will be found with more details (*luculentius*).

* Que esperava algun dia escrivir algo por memoria de su amo, lo qual dezia que no havia aun empezado por haver estado por acá siempre achacoso y doliente. — *Papiers d'Etat du Cardinal de Granvelle,* vi. p. 290.

† Herus meus. — *Lettres de Guillaume van Male,* p. 47. Su amo. — *Papiers d'Etat de Granvelle,* vi. p. 290.

‡ He sabido que mucho ántes que muriesse, rasgó y quemó muchos papeles, y que viviendo se havia quexado muchas vezes à algunos amigos suyas. — *State Papers of Cardinal de Granvelle,* vi. p. 290.

repeatedly conversed respecting this work,
which would have fulfilled the dream and
desire of his whole life.* Incontestably these
rumours, these intentions, found an echo in
other countries, which had also been witnesses of
the exploits of Charles V., and no astonishment
can be felt if they were known in Italy.
Venice, whose affairs were, according to Co-
mines, 'more wisely managed than by any other
living prince,' was not ignorant of anything
which occurred in Europe. In 1559, Marco-
Antonio da Mula was sent on an extraordinary
mission of the Republic to the Netherlands, and
each day its merchants exchanged long letters
between Antwerp, the Queen of the Scheldt, and
Venice, the Queen of the Adriatic.

At the very hour Van Male was breathing
his last, a Venetian gentleman, Louis Dolce, observes in a life of Charles V. that he was a good
French scholar.

* It was probably only after the return of Van Male to the
Netherlands that the report was spread in various quarters that
Charles V. had dictated his Commentaries, and that they
were to be translated into Latin. In 1559, Zenocarus is still
ignorant of their existence, but, however, he alleges, in denial,
the considerations which alarmed the conscience of Charles V. :
' Veritus ne laudis propriæ avidus à Deo censeretur.'

It is said (he adds) that he composed in that language some very fine commentaries of the acts which he had performed, and, as I am informed, they are actually being translated into Latin, and will be published.*

All Italy was still full of the memory of Charles V., and both Bernardo Tasso, whose illustrious son called glory the shadow of a dream, and Girolamo Ruscelli, who had for a long time been engaged in collecting biographies of illustrious men, entertained the idea of writing his history. Ruscelli repeated what Dolce had said, giving more or less exactly the name of the translator : —

It is hoped that the Commentaries translated into Latin by William Marinde will shortly appear.

Dolce had announced that a translation was under preparation. Ruscelli, who wrote from the same city, and at the same period, goes farther : he asserts that it is being printed. It

---

* Alcuni bellissimi commentari delle cose da lui fatte, i quali, come odo, hora si traducono in latino e si darano fuori.

In 1565 Dolce published a new edition of his book. The sentence which refers to the Commentaries of Charles V., which is both vague and ambiguous, was not modified. Nothing farther was known at Venice from 1561 to 1565.

is doubtful whether any such translation ever was made, but it appears to us perfectly inadmissible that it was actually sent to the press at Venice. Would William van Male, who had received the appointment of Major-Domo of the palace at Brussels, and drew a pension, have dared surreptitiously to make a publication at Venice which would have called down upon him the anger of Philip II.?* The whole, moreover, is reduced to the very suspicious authority of Brantôme, who has exaggerated, without understanding them, the data collected by Dolce and Ruscelli: —

It is said that the great Emperor wrote a book with his own hand, as Julius Cæsar did in Latin. I do not know whether he did so, but I have seen a letter published amongst those of Belleforest, which he has translated from Italian into French, which testifies to it having been turned into Latin by William Marinde; which I cannot quite believe, as all the world would have hastened to buy a copy, like bread in time of famine; and certainly the

* We should be more inclined to admit that the reports spread at Venice contributed to the search which took place amongst Van Male's papers after his death. 'He entendido,' wrote Philip II. to Cardinal de Granvelle, when he sent him the order to make the search without delay.

desire of possessing so great and rare a book would have made the price very high, and everyone would have liked to have his own copy.

For three centuries, with the exception of the vague indication of an impression said to have been made at Hanau at the commencement of the seventeenth century, under the auspices of a son-in-law of William the Silent,* all the questions which refer to the translation of William van Male have remained veiled in the same darkness; but these very mysteries seem to have added to the interest, and it must be stated to the honour of the country of Charles V., that the first learned body of Belgium has taken the most prominent part in

* Teissier, who has been copied by all those who have spoken of the edition of the *Commentaries of Charles V. at Hanau,* confines himself to say — 'Carolus Quintus scripsit de propria vita libellum qui prodiit Hanoviæ, 1602.' But is there not an error here, which may very easily be explained if we substitute the name of the Emperor Charles IV. for Charles V.? In fact a life of Charles IV., written by himself, was published at Hanau in 1602, and is to be found in a collection of the historians of Bohemia. I am indebted for this information to Dr. Hoffmann of Hamburg. The collection is that of Marquard Freher, and the life of Charles IV. is thus designated:— 'Caroli Bohemiæ regis et postea imperatoris de vita sua commentarius ab ipso scriptus.' It seems to me very difficult not to recognise in this title of a work published at Hanau in 1602 the source of Teissier's mistake.

the efforts that have been made to fill up the blank.

In 1845, M. Gachard, whose name will always remain associated to the researches which have spread so bright a light upon the history of the sixteenth century, entertained the Royal Academy of Belgium with his investigations at Simancas, at the Escurial, and at Madrid, respecting ' a document, the discovery of which would have excited universal interest; ' and he dwelt upon how much was to be regretted ' the loss of those memoirs traced by the hand of the most powerful of monarchs, and perhaps of the most profound political genius of the sixteenth century.' Fourteen years which the learned Keeper-General of the Archives of the Kingdom had devoted to new studies, which had remained fruitless on one single point, though so fruitful on every other, had passed by, when the examination of the same question was taken up by M. Arendt, in a notice which attracted public attention in the highest degree.

Assuredly the honour of discovering the ' Commentaries of Charles V.' is due legitimately to my honourable colleagues of the Royal

Academy of Belgium, and if a chance has decided it otherwise, it is doubtless that we should
have it in our power here to proclaim all that
is due to their excellent labours.

Moreover, we hasten to say so ;. we have not
had the good fortune to disinter the actual
text of the Commentaries of the celebrated
Emperor. We have simply discovered a translation in the Portuguese language, — a translation which was the only work in the southern
tongue inscribed in the great inventory (*grand
inventaire du fond français*) at the Imperial
Library at Paris, where, however, a reference
is given to the Spanish division, No. 10,230.
It is this error which probably has so long con-
cealed it from the curious eye of researchers.*

The manuscript, which is in elegant and
polished handwriting, bears the following
title : —

'*Historia del invictissimo Emperador Carlos-*

* My researches at Paris were connected with the publication of various of our ancient authors of the fifteenth century,
which was intrusted to me by the Academy. I cannot sufficiently acknowledge the obliging kindness with which MM. the
Guardians of the Imperial Library facilitated my numerous
investigations.

*Quinto, Rey de Hespanha, composta por Sua
Majestade Cesarea, como se vee do papel que vai
em a seguinte folha, traduzida da lingoa francesa
e do proprio original, em Madrid, anno* 1620.'

That is to say : —

'The History of the most invincible Emperor
Charles V., King of Spain, composed by his Imperial
Majesty (or his Cesarean Majesty, as Brantôme
styles him), as is shown by the paper on the following page, translated from the French, and from the
original at Madrid in 1620.'

Thus in 1620, in the reign of Philip III. and
under the ministry of the Duke d'Uzeda, the
original manuscript of the Commentaries still
existed at Madrid: what has become of it since?
Did some prejudice of national honour cause
it to be destroyed when the grandson of a
King of France came to occupy the throne of
Charles V.? Has it been the foot-ball at the
commencement of this century of some of those
soldiers, who little thought they were avenging
the vanquished of Pavia when they made their
weapons clang in the caverns of the Escurial,
where reposes the rival of Francis I.? Or is
it, on the contrary, preserved amongst a lot of

secret archives? Spain, we hope, will deem these doubts worthy of solution.

However, the weakness and the decay of the monarchy under Philip III. may explain, at the same time, how the public mind looked back with a feeling of sorrow and regret toward the reign of Charles V., and how the documents which remained hidden from the Sandovals and Sepulvedas were allowed to be seen by the *Coronistes*, their successors. In 1623, Gilles Gonzalez d'Avila, Historiographer of Philip III., again affirmed the existence of the Commentaries, and perhaps he saw them. The translation into Portuguese is easily explained.* Portugal was still united to Spain, and it was about the same period that Francis d'Andrada and Antonio de Souza wrote in Portuguese the 'Life of King John III.,' so intimately connected with that of Charles V. It will have been seen that our manuscript announced a note which was to establish its authenticity. It is, in fact, to be

---

* If a publication did take place at Hanau, and if it is posterior to 1602, as would be supposed by seeing it mentioned for the first time in a catalogue of 1705, would it not have been in the Portuguese language? Emmanuel of Portugal married, in 1646, a daughter of the Count of Hanau.

found in the second sheet, and is conceived in
these terms :—

*'Treslado do papel que esta em o principio desta
historia, escritto per mão propria do Emperador
Carlos V. em a lingoa Castelhana, o qual papel
Sua Majestade mandou d'Alemanha com a mesma
historia a el rey Don Philippe seu filho que entāõ
era principe de Hespanha.'*

Which translated means :—

'Copy of a paper placed at the commencement of
this history, which was written in Spanish in the
manu-proprio of the Emperor Charles V., and
which was sent to Germany with this same history,
by His Majesty, to his son the King Philip, then
still Prince of Spain.'

Immediately afterwards follow a few lines
addressed by Charles V. to the Prince of Spain,
and they give a summary of the history of the
composition of the Commentaries. As we learn
from Van Male's recital, they were commenced
on the Rhine when Charles V. went up it with
his son,* then completed at Augsburg, which
confirms the ingenious conjectures of M. Arendt.
Charles V. protests his good faith, which modern

* Quando venimos.

historians are disposed to admit. He declares that he has not written from vanity, and we know how all his historiographers attribute the honour to him of having been at the same time great and modest in his successes.* In addressing posterity he places himself under the eye of God. It is God whom he invokes to grant him time to complete his work, that it may serve His glory; it is under the protection of God that he hopes to be delivered from his anxieties and troubles, the trace of which is to be found in these unfinished lines.

Here we are on the threshold of the Commentaries. The reader is doubtless impatient to pass it, and we shall content ourselves with adding to this introduction a few words, not to judge the work of Charles V., but to explain, under the circumstances when it was written, what it ought to be, and what in fact it is.

For the more distant period, the Emperor, assisted by Van Male,† and attaching himself

---

* Inania gloriæ et falsæ laudis contemptor. — *Sepulveda.*

† Quâ in re usus est operâ meâ et suggestione, nam velut nomenclator revocabam in memoriam si quid sentirem aut effluere aut prætermitti. — *Lettres de Guillaume van Male,* p. 12.

especially to dates and facts, is satisfied with
grouping some details together, and enume-
rating his numerous crossings of the sea, which
he alluded to so eloquently in his abdication
speech, when drawing a brilliant picture of the
past, combining with them the cold and sombre
images of the future, and pointing out what
would be the last. But as soon as he touches
upon the era of the memorable campaigns in
France and Germany, we recognise in the
narrator as great a skill in strategy as in
politics. Despite the obstacles multiplied by
the violent attacks of his enemies or by their
disguised subterfuges, he, unaided, sufficed for
that task, too immense, as Mignet observes,
for one man; and it is especially in these Commentaries that he will be found firm in his convictions and in his projects, and struggling
courageously, though infirm and ill, against the
most formidable leagues, and against the most
audacious outburst of the liberty of the human
mind, which discarded all principle of authority.

As regards the form, it is a methodical narration without adornment, in which perhaps may
be discovered some imitation of the immortal

work of Cæsar.* It recalls the assertion of
Sepulveda, that the Emperor loved truth in all
its simplicity :—

'simplicis veritatis amantissimus.'

We have endeavoured to preserve to him that
character, by following a system contrary to
that of Van Male, by faithfully reproducing the
sense and even the phraseology of the narration
which we have before us. The importance of
this historical document, which we only know
by a first translation, appeared to us to demand
that the one which we now publish should renounce elegance of style to be the more faithful.

It would have been an easy task for us to
add numerous notes to every page, and to
compare the narrative of the Emperor with
that of contemporary historians. We have not
done so out of respect to his memory. It is
said that Don Louis d'Avila, in his retreat at
Placentia, had placed between the busts of

---

* Charles V., like Cæsar, speaks of himself only in the third
person, and the opinion of Cicero upon the Commentaries of the
conqueror of Gaul must not be forgotten :—' Commentarios
quosdam scripsit rerum suarum, valde probandos. Nudi enim
sunt, recti et venusti, omni ornatu orationis detracto. Nihil
enim est, in historia, pura et illustri brevitate dulcius.'

Augustus and Antoninus that of Charles V., with this inscription : —

> '*Carolo Quinto—ed è assai questo.*'

(To Charles V.—that name suffices.)

Like Louis d'Avila, we think that, after having announced the Commentaries of Charles V., there is nothing to be added to the title. It is just that the voice of the Prince, whom the faithful Quijada called 'the greatest man that ever lived or ever will live,' should be heard after three centuries of silence, free and unshackled by murmurs and contradictors. At a later period history will resume her rights, but henceforth, before appreciating the political career of Charles V., it will be necessary to study his own judgement of it at a moment when, the better to interrogate his conscience, he was preparing voluntarily to relinquish the most vast power that ever was known.

CHARLES V.

TO HIS SON

PHILIP PRINCE OF SPAIN.

———◦◦◦———

THIS history is that which I composed in French, when we were travelling on the Rhine, and which I finished at Augsburg. It is not such as I could wish it, but God knows that I did not do it out of vanity, and if He has been offended at it, my offence must be attributed rather to ignorance than to malice. Similar things have often provoked His anger : I should not like this to rouse His ire against me! In these circumstances, as in others, reasons will not be wanting to Him. May He moderate His anger, and deliver me from the dilemma in which I see myself!

I was on the point of throwing the whole into the fire ; but, as I hope, if God gives me

life to arrange this history in such guise that
He shall not find Himself ill served therein,
and that it may not run the risk of being lost
here, I send it to you that you may have it
kept down there, and that it may not be
opened until *　.　.　.

I THE KING.

Inspruck, 1552.

* Esta historia es la que yo hize en romance, quando venimos
por el Rin, y la acabé en Augusta. Ella no está hecha como queria,
y Dios sabe que no la hize con vanidad, y si della él se tuvo por
ofendido, mi ofensa fué mas por ignorancia que por malicia. Por
cosas semejantes, él se solia mucho enojar: no querria que por esta
lo uviesse hecho agora conmigo. Ansi por esta como por otras
ocasiones, no le faltarán causas. Plega á él de templar su yra, y
sacarme del trabajo en que me veo. Yo estuve por quemarlo todo;
mas porque, si Dios me da vida, confio ponerla de manera que él no
se deservirá della, para que por acá no ande en peligro de perderse,
os la embio para que por acá no ande en peligro de perderse, os la
embio para que agays que allá sea guardada, y no abierta hasta. . .

Yo El Rey.

En Inspruck, 1552.

AUTOBIOGRAPHY OF CHARLES V.

CHAPTER I.

War in Flanders.—League between the Emperor Maximilian and
Henry of England against the King of France. —Capture of
Terouane.—Surrender of Tournay.—Charles assumes the Title of
King 1516.—He assembles the Cortes of the Kingdoms of Castille
at Valladolid. —Death of the Emperor Maximilian. —Charles is
elected Emperor.—Visits England.—Has an interview with Henry
VIII.—Visits Flanders.—Commencement of the Reformation.—
Luther.—War with France.—Siege of Pavia.—Visits England a
second time. —Francis I. is made Prisoner. —The battle of
Bicocca.—Capture of Genoa.—Peace with France.—Birth of Philip
Prince of Spain (1527).—The Pope made a Prisoner.

AFTER the death of King Philip, there were at
intervals various wars in the States of Flanders,
which we call the Netherlands. One of those wars
was that undertaken by the Emperor Maximilian, in
concert with King Henry of England, against Louis,
King of France. By the prudence, as well as by the
habitual bravery of the Emperor,* the French were

* Pola prudencia como polo esforço costumado do Emperador.

B 2

defeated whilst endeavouring to relieve Terouane. After the capture of that city, siege was laid to Tournay, which, shortly afterwards, also surrendered. The result was, that the Archduke Charles, grandson of the Emperor, proceeded to Tournay, which was then in the hands of King Henry, and to Lille, where he had his first interview with the same King, and where, amongst other things, his emancipation was discussed and resolved upon. This took place 1515 in the year 1515, during which he was immediately recognised as Lord of the said States of Flanders. Shortly afterwards, the same Archduke sent ambassadors to King Francis of France, who at the same period had inherited that kingdom, on the death of King Louis. These ambassadors negotiated and concluded peace. In the same year, His Majesty visited a portion of the States of Flanders, and whilst making that visit, there arrived at the Hague, in Holland, M. de Vendôme, sent by the King of France to ratify that peace. That portion of his States which he had not time to visit this year, was visited by him in the 1516 following year, 1516, and he held his first Chapter of the Order of the Golden Fleece at Brussels. This was the year of the death of the Catholic King; and, dating from that moment, the Archduke assumed the title of King.*

---

* E d'entaõ por diante o Archiduque tomou o titulo de Rey.

At the same period he recovered, not without some resistance, his domains in Friesland: then the King of France, on the occasion of his recent accession, expressed a desire to open other negotiations with His Majesty,* which took place at Noyon, at the same time and in the same year. The King of France sent the Seigneur d'Orval to ratify what had been newly agreed upon. His Majesty remained in the Netherlands until September 8, 1517, upon 1517 which day he embarked at Flushing for Spain, and he left for the first time, in his absence, Margaret, his aunt, Governor of his States.

This same year, His Majesty maintaining the peace concluded in France, and the friendship of the King of England,† embarked, as already stated, at Flushing, crossed the ocean, and for the first time saw Spain, where his sojourn was to be prolonged till 1520. Continuing his journey to Tordesillas, he went to kiss the hands of the Queen his mother, and starting from thence, he proceeded to Mojados, where he met the Infant Don Ferdinand, his brother, whom he welcomed with great fraternal love.‡ At this time Cardinal Fray Francis Ximenes, whom the Catholic King had instituted Governor of

---

* Despois el Rey de França desejou de trattar de novo com Sua Majestade, por causa da nova successaõ.

† Continuando a paz feita em França e amizade com el Rey d'Inglaterra.

‡ Com grande e fraternal amor.

his kingdoms, died. Continuing his journey, His
Majesty arrived at Valladolid, where he assembled
the Cortes of the kingdoms of Castille; and he was
recognised as King conjointly with the Queen his
mother.*

At this time the King of France intimated to His
Majesty a certain intention and wish to go to war
with the King of England, to recover, he said, the
town of Tournay, which, as has been seen, had been
captured. To which His Majesty replied in terms
in keeping with the conventions he had concluded
with the two Kings. This reply, though moderate,
just, and reasonable, was interpreted in such guise
that the King of France felt insulted, and, shortly
afterwards, he commenced war. On the other hand,
the English monarch did not display the gratitude
which such a reply deserved. For soon the tw
Kings came to an agreement, and formed an alliance, taking little into account the conventions which
had been concluded between them and the Catholic
King. In consequence of this agreement and this
alliance, the town of Tournay was restored to the
French.†

---

* E foi jurado por Rey juntamente com a Rainha sua mai.

† El Rey de França fez advertir a Sua Magestade de certa tenção
sua e vontade que tinha de fazer guerra ao Rey d'Inglaterra por
cobrar, segundo dizia, a Tornay que, como dantes se disse, fora
tomada. Ao que Sua Magestade respondeo conforme os concertos,
que tinha feitos com os dittos dous Reys. A qual resposta, ainda

At this time, that is to say in the year 1518, His 1518
Majesty, and the Infant his brother, left Valladolid,
for Saragossa; and during this journey he parted
company with the Infant at Aranda, who, leaving
that town, embarked at Santander, going by sea to
Flanders, where he was received by Madam his aunt.
His Majesty continued his journey to Saragossa,
where, in the same manner, he convoked the Cortes,
and was recognised as King.*

In the year 1519 His Majesty assembled the 1519
Cortes at Barcelona, where the same ceremony took
place. On his way he learnt the death of the
Emperor Maximilian, his grandfather; and, whilst
holding the Cortes, the news reached him of his
election to the Empire, which Duke Frederick, Count
Palatine, was charged to announce to him. From
thence he left for Corunna, to embark to receive the
Imperial Crown at Aix-la-Chapelle.†

His Majesty embarked at Corunna, leaving as
governor Cardinal de Tortosa, to whom he afterwards gave as adjuncts the Constable and the Ad-
miral of Castille, Don Inigo de Velasco, and Don

---

que branda, justa, e conforme a razáõ, foi tomaða de sorte que el
Rey de França se resentio tee pouco despois começar a guerra, e o
Ingrez não teve o reconhecimento que a tal resposta merecia, porque
logo se concertaram e unirao ambos, fazendo pouco caso dos concertos, que estavam feitos entre elles e o Rey Catholico.

* Onde da mesma maneira ajuntou cortes, e foi jurado por Rey.
† A primeira corõa.

Frederick Henriquez. Having crossed the ocean a second time, he landed for the first time in England, where he had his second interview with the King, and, despite what has been said above, a closer alliance was negotiated and concluded with the said King.* From thence he crossed over to his States of Flanders, where he was received by Madam his aunt, and by the Infant his brother. This was the first return of His Majesty to his States of Flanders : a third interview was the result, at Gravelines and at Calais, between the Emperor and King Henry of England. He then continued his journey to Aix-la-Chapelle, where he was crowned. He again appointed Margaret his aunt Governor of Flanders; he also left his brother the Infant there, and held his first Diet at Worms. This is the first time that he visited Germany and the Rhine. About this time the heretical doctrines of Luther in Germany, and the *Communidades* in Spain, began to manifest themselves.†

His Majesty, being at the said Diet, sent for his brother, who from thence went to marry the sister of King Louis of Hungary, according to what had been settled by the Emperor Maximilian.

During this same Diet, Robert de la Mark com-

---

* Mais particular paz.

† Começaram a pullular as heregias de Luthero em Alemanha e as communidades em Hespanha.

menced hostilities.* This act had its origin in the reply, mentioned above, which in 1518 the Catholic King Charles had addressed from Valladolid to the King of France. Not only could that King not conceal his mortification and little satisfaction it gave him, but it gradually increased, especially when the Catholic King was elected Emperor.†

He was continually making complaints and such unreasonable proposals, and in such exorbitant terms, that the Emperor could neither accept them nor condescend to notice them.‡ From this reason and from other practices, and other communications which the King of France entertained in Italy and in Spain with the *Communidades*,§ war commenced in 1521 between His Majesty and the King of France, in which Robert de la Mark lost the greater portion of his domains, which were taken from him by Count Henry of Nassau, then Captain-General of the army. These wars lasted till 1525. For this reason the Emperor was obliged to close the Diet at Worms. By so acting, he rather did what he could

* Começou a mover guerra.

† Da qual não soo mente não pode dissimular o desgosto e pouca satisfação que tinha, mas cada dia ia em crescimento, e muito mais despois que o ditto Rey Catholico foi eleito em Emperador.

‡ E lhe foram continuamente feitos requerimentos, e postas condições táõ desarrezoádas e per termos táõ exorbitantes que não pode oir, nem condescender nellas.

§ Pola qual causa, e outtras pratticas e intelligencias que havia em Italia, e em Hespanha com as communidades.

than what he wished and had resolved to do,* and he left to oppose those hostilities.

1521   His Majesty returned by the Rhine, into his States of Flanders for the second time. At this period the *Communidades* were suppressed in Spain, and the French beaten and‚ driven out of the kingdom of Navarre, which they had occupied ‚in like manner as they had established themselves at Fontarabia. All these things occurred before the close of the year.

At this time the King of France sent an army into Lombardy. It laid siege to Pavia, which was defended by the Marquis Frederick of Mantua. An army having been assembled, in virtue of the league entered into by the Emperor with Pope Leo and the Venetians, the French were driven out of the Duchy of Milan. Prosper Colonna was chief of the army of the League; and, in virtue of the same League, the Duchy of Milan was given to Duke Francis Sforza.

At the same time, by the Emperor's orders, the Count of Nassau laid siege to the town of Tournay, which was surrendered by the French to His Majesty, who had occupied it since they received it from the King of England, into whose power it had previously fallen. The army of the King of
1522 France again attempted, in 1522, to reenter the Duchy of Milan, but Prosper Colonna and the army of the League made so valiant a resistance that the

* Mais como pode que como desejava e determinava fazer.

French lost the battle of Bicocca. The capture of Genoa followed.

The Emperor, for the third time, leaving the government of Flanders to his aunt, embarked at Calais, and, for the second time, visited England, where he had his fourth interview with the King. Having remained there some days, he embarked at Southampton, crossed the ocean for the third time, and arrived a second time in Spain, where he again went to kiss the hands of his mother the Queen, and where he remained till 1529. At the very time of his arrival, Pope Adrian, who had been elected on the death of Pope Leo, embarked at Barcelona for Rome. His Majesty continued his journey to Valladolid, where he assembled the Cortes to complete the reconciliation of past differences, excepting a few of the more culpable from the general pardon granted to all those who had offended him.

In the year 1523, during the war with France, the 1523 Emperor entertained certain communications and certain correspondence * with Duke Charles of Bourbon, who felt himself injured by some acts of injustice done towards him.† This is why he entered the service of His Imperial Majesty. The Emperor proceeding to Pampeluna with an army to invade

---

* Teve algúa communicáõ e intelligencia.

† O qual se tinha por injuriado de algús aggravos que lhe foram feitos.

France, gave the command of it to Don Inigo de
Velasco, Constable of Castille, who penetrated into the
kingdom, and who on his return recaptured Fontarabia.

1524   This achieved, the Emperor returned in 1524 to
the kingdom of Toledo. He was taken ill with fever,
1525 which he got rid of early in the following year, 1525.
At this time the King of France laid siege to Pavia,
which was held by Antonio de Leyva, and, in the
battle fought in front of that city, the King was
made prisoner by the Duke of Bourbon,* Captain-
General of the Emperor, Charles de Lannoy, his
Viceroy at Naples, and Don Francis d'Avalos,
Marquis of Pescaria, his principal captains. The
King was taken by the Viceroy of Naples into Spain
to Madrid, where he fell sick, and the Emperor
went to pay him a visit. This is the first time they
met.

Whilst the Emperor was in the said city of Madrid,
peace was negotiated and concluded with the said
King, and his marriage with the Queen-widow of
Portugal, Eleanor, sister of the Emperor. At the
same time the Duke of Bourbon also arrived, who
returned soon to Milan, having been invested with
that state by His Majesty.

1526   In 1526 the Emperor left Toledo for Seville,

---

* Pelo dantes ditto duque de Borbon.

where he married. On his journey, he received the news of the death of his sister the Queen of Denmark. In the same city of Seville, he was visited by his brother-in-law, the Infant Don Louis of Portugal, who accompanied the Empress his sister. This was the first time His Majesty saw the said Infant. At the same time he set at liberty the King of France,* receiving in exchange two of his sons as hostages, conformable to the conditions of the conventions made at Madrid. The latter, shortly afterwards, renewed the war, and His Imperial Majesty received a message of defiance † at Grenada, consequent upon a league concluded between Pope Clement, who had been elected on the demise of Adrian, the Kings of France and of England, and the Signoria of Venice. His Majesty sent a reply to that defiance.

In the same city the news reached the Emperor that his brother-in-law, King Louis of Hungary, had been defeated by the Turks and had perished. This is why His Majesty convoked the general Cortes of all his kingdoms of Castille, to concert measures to remedy such a state of things, and to organise the necessary means of defence against the Turks. His Majesty was in this city, in 1527, when his son Philip 1527 Prince of Spain was born. About the same time, and in the same city, he received the news that the army raised by the Duke of Bourbon had entered

* Soltou. † Foi desafiado.

Rome, after an assault, in which the said Duke was killed, and that Pope Clement was shut up * in the fort of St. Angelo. A guard was placed in the fort by the Prince of Orange, who, after the death of the Duke of Bourbon, took command of the army.

The Pope remained in the said fortress until, having come to terms with the army,† he was by His Majesty's orders set at liberty.

At the same time, in the city of Burgos, the Emperor received a message of defiance from the Kings of France and of England, under the pretext of the detention of Pope Clement.‡ His Majesty replied that there were no grounds for such an act, as the Pope had already been liberated; and that the fact of the detention of the Pope ought to be reproached less to the Emperor than to those who had compelled him to raise for his defence so many soldiers who did not obey him well.§

All this having taken place, His Majesty returned to Madrid, where he convoked the Cortes of the kingdoms of Castille, where his son Philip was recognised ‖ Prince of the said kingdoms. In the year 1528, His Majesty, on his way to Valladolid,

1528

---

* Encerrado.

† Tee que tendo se concertado com o exercito.

‡ Sob color da detençáò do papa Clemente.

§ E o que tinha acontecido de sua detençáò fora mais por culpa daquelles o obrigaram a mandar para sua defensáò tanta gente de guerra que não foi bem obedecido, que por sua.

‖ Foi jurado.

experienced a first attack of gout. He received the
news that an army sent by the King of France into
Italy, under the pretext of delivering Pope Clement,
(who, as has already been said, had been liberated,) * had advanced to invade and attack the
kingdom of Naples; that it had already conquered a
large portion of it, and had laid siege to the capital,
into which the army which was before Rome had
withdrawn. In that army were the Prince of
Orange, Don Alphonso d'Avalos, the Marquis du
Guast, Alarcon, who had occupied the castle of St.
Angelo, and Don Hugo de Moncada, who was in
the said city of Naples, happening to be there at the
time of the death of the Viceroy Charles de Lannoy;
and as each laid claim to the supreme command,
they were not on very good terms with each other.
Nevertheless they performed their duty so well that,
with God's blessing, the said kingdom and capital
were defended, and the French army vanquished
and routed.† During this siege, Don Hugo de
Moncada attacked the galleys belonging to the
squadron of Prince Doria; but Hugo de Moncada
was killed, and most of his galleys captured.

His Majesty, conformably to the resolution he
had taken, proceeded to Monzon to hold the Cortes
of the three kingdoms of Aragon. This done, he

---

* Com cor de querer livrar o papa Clemente, o qual, como fica
ditto, estava ja livre. † Rotto e desbaratado.

returned to Madrid, where the Empress was residing,
who had given birth to the Infanta Doña Maria, her
first daughter. Soon after envoys arrived from
Prince Doria, who, from certain reasons and bad
treatment he had received,* offered to join His
Majesty with his galleys and with those he had captured at Naples. His Majesty willingly accepted
the offer, which was most welcome to him, and indispensable for the success of the plans he had in view.†

From this city the Emperor proceeded to Toledo;
and in this town he charged the Empress to govern
in his absence all his Spanish dominions, which he
resolved to leave, animated by the desire of counter-
acting as much as possible the errors in Germany
which, owing to the wars he had been engaged in,
he had only been able to remedy imperfectly.‡ He
also wished, by resisting the attacks incessantly
directed against him on the Italian side, at the same
time to assume the crowns which he had not yet
received, and finally to be in a better position to
oppose the Turk, who, it was said, was advancing
against Christendom.

From these various motives the Emperor left the

---

* Por alguas causas e mao trattamento que lhe fora feito.

† O qual Sua Majestade acceitou de boa vontade por este offerecimento lhe ser de muito gosto e necessario para o que trattava fazer
e que cada dia se lhe podia offerecer.

‡ Po lo desejo que tinha de dar a melhor ordem que lhe fosse
possivel aos erros antes dittos de Alemanha que, como esta ditto, Sua
Majestade deixara o remedio imperfeito.

city of Toledo for Barcelona, where Prince Doria
shortly afterwards arrived with his galleys. Here
he got his fleet into order so as to embark, as
already stated, and have himself crowned in Italy,
despite the league already mentioned which had been
formed against His Majesty, and which, at the same
moment, was beginning to break up: for, whilst he
was still at Barcelona, negotiations were set on
foot between Pope Clement and His Majesty. Here
the news came that M. de Saint Pol had been
defeated in the states of Milan, and that he was the
prisoner of Antonio de Leyva, Governor of those
states. At the same time, his aunt Margaret was
negotiating at Cambray a peace with the Queen
Regent of France, mother of the King. This done,
His Majesty embarked and set sail with his whole
fleet, landing for the first time in Italy. Whilst
cruising along the French coast, he received the
report that peace had been concluded; but he only
received the confirmation of it on his arrival at
Savona. He consequently sent Seigneur de la
Chaulx, one of his household, from Genoa to ratify it.
From Genoa he proceeded farther into Italy, where
he learnt that the Turks had entered Hungary and
laid siege to Vienna. This led to the first interview
between Pope Clement and the Emperor at Bologna,
where His Majesty experienced a second attack of gout.

C

CHAPTER II.

Birth of a Second Son.—Concludes Peace with Venice.—Death of the Prince of Orange.— Siege of Vienna by the Turks.—Convocation of a Diet at Augsburg.—The King of the Romans.—Holds a Chapter of the Golden Fleece.—The Diet at Ratisbon.—Defeat of the Turks.— Interview with the Pope.— Holds the Cortes at Monzon.—Expedition to Tunis.— Pope Paul succeeds Clement.— Barbarossa.— Sack of Tunis.—Visits Italy a third time. — Death of the Queen of England.—Interview with Pope Paul (1536).—Antonio de Leyva.—The Count de Buren. – Capture of Montreuil.—Peace with France. –Is attacked by French Galleys.

AT Bologna the Emperor was informed that the Empress had given birth to a second son, Ferdinand, whose death was announced to him the following year at Augsburg. To be more free to oppose the Turks and to leave Italy tranquil,* he assumed the crowns that belonged to him, in the said city of Bologna.†

He concluded peace with the Venetians, and again intrusted the states of Milan to Francesco Sforza. After a long war waged by the Pope and His Majesty against the Florentines, in which the Prince of

* E por Sua Majestade ficar mais livre parar resistir ao Turco e per deixar Italia quieta.
† Suas Coroas.

Orange, who was already Viceroy of Naples, fulfilled
the functions of Captain-General, the House of the
Medici was reestablished in Florence, and Duke
Alexander invested with that state. In this expedition the Prince of Orange was killed. He was
replaced in his command by Don Ferdinand de
Gonzaga, and in the government of Naples by Cardinal Caracciolo, until His Majesty should decree
otherwise.

Meantime so valiant a resistance was made by the
King his brother, and by those who were with him
at Vienna, that the Turk, as well from this reason
as from the information he received of the great
preparations that were being made to oppose him,
thought fit to withdraw. At the same time the
Emperor asked His Holiness to convoke and assemble
a general council, as most important and necessary to
remedy what was taking place in Germany, and the
errors which were being propagated throughout
Christendom.* To this effect His Holiness appointed
a Legate to attend the Diet at Augsburg, and there
to adopt all such resolutions as might seem best
suited for such an object.

These matters settled, the Emperor, taking leave 1530

---

* Como de cousa mais principal e necessaria, o Emperador solli-
citou a Sua Santitade que, para remedio da Germania e dos erros
que iáo multiplicando em a Christandade, quisesse, como unico e
principal remedio, convocar e celebrar hum concilio geral.

of the Pope, left Bologna to proceed to the Diet
which he had convoked at Augsburg. Here he was
joined by the Pope's Legate to consider the remedies
for the said errors, and at the same time to provide
for and obviate the evils which were feared on the
part of the Turk. The Emperor, passing through
Mantua and the territories of Venice, arrived at
Trent and in Germany for the second time. During
this voyage he met the King his brother, and they
proceeded together to the said Diet of Augsburg,
where good measures were concerted against the
Turk, which were afterwards carried out at Ratisbon. At this time he entered into negotiations
with the electors.* As the Emperor, because of the
great kingdoms and large domains which God had
given to him, could not prolong his sojourn in the
empire as long as he desired and was suitable,† the
question of the election of his brother as King of the
Romans was brought forward. On the closing of the
Diet they all started together, and for the third time
the Emperor visited the Rhine, following it up to
Cologne. It was here that (owing to the plague
prevailing at Frankfort) the election of the King
his brother as King of the Romans was concluded on
1531 the proposition of His Majesty. From the said city
of Cologne the Emperor proceeded to Aix-la-Cha-

---

* Prattica et intelligencia.   † Quanto desejeva e convinha,

pelle to crown the said King. This being done, the
King and the electors commenced treating their
private interests, and the Emperor returned a third
time into his states of Flanders to put things into
order there, as well on account of his long absence, as
in consequence of the death of Margaret, his aunt,
the news of which reached him on his journey down
the Rhine. So as to place everything in the best
order, he intrusted the management and direction of
affairs to his sister, the Queen of Hungary. This
having been all settled and completed, he made a
tour through his states, visiting a portion of his
domains. It was with the assistance and in company
of the said Queen that he took all the measures that
appeared to him most suitable and most necessary.
Amongst other things he held a third chapter of the
order of the Golden Fleece at Tournay.

At the commencement of this year the Emperor, 1532
leaving for the first time the Queen of Hungary, his
sister, in the government of the said states of Flanders,
started the fourth time for the Rhine, so as to enter
Germany a third time, as well as to see whether he
could not hit upon some means of putting a stop to
the heresies that were spreading there* as to oppose
the invasion of the Turk, who, as was announced, was
preparing to invade Germany with a great army.

* Por ver se podia fazer algũa cousa de proveito para remedio das
heregias que havia nella.

For this purpose the Emperor convoked an Imperial
Diet at Ratisbon, to carry into execution what had
been agreed upon, as has already been said, at
Augsburg. During this journey, whilst out hunting,
he had a fall from his horse and hurt his leg; ery-
sipelas having ensued, he suffered from it the whole
time he was at Ratisbon. He also experienced a
third attack of gout. His nephew the Prince of
Denmark died in the same city.

Whilst His Majesty was thus laid up, the Diet
discussed what remedy could be applied to the state
of religious matters, and the certain news arrived of
the advance of the Turk with the object mentioned
above. For this reason, His Majesty, conjointly
with the King of the Romans, his brother, appealed
to the states of the empire, who showed themselves
full of zeal in the performance of their duty.
Religious matters were therefore left aside, as there
was no time to discuss them,* and they were left
in their actual state. Such an army was assembled by the empire, as well as by their Majesties
the Emperor and the King of the Romans that
the Turk, who wished to besiege Vienna, where
the Emperor and the King of the Romans had
anticipated him with their troops, finding that a
portion of his troops which had advanced on different

* Pola brevidade do tempo.

army, commanded by General Marquis du Guast.
After being delayed by some skirmishes, he besieged
Goulette for some days with heavy artillery,* and
finally carried it by storm.

At this time the Emperor received the news that
the Empress had given birth to the Infanta Doña
Juana, her second daughter. A few days afterwards,
leaving Goulette and the fleet well provided for, he
advanced towards Tunis with his infantry and cavalry
and some pieces of artillery. Whilst advancing,
Barbarossa made a sortie from Tunis with a large
body of Moors on horse and foot, supported by numerous artillery, and attacked the Emperor between
some pits and swamps, where he had halted to rest
his army.

The Emperor took possession of the ground, and
compelled the enemy to withdraw, with the loss of
their artillery and of a portion of their troops. His
Majesty also suffered some loss on his side; on the
same day Barbarossa beat a retreat toward Tunis.
At daybreak next morning, the Emperor drew up
his army in order of battle and advanced against
the said city of Tunis, and neither Barbarossa nor
his men could prevent him forcing an entrance
with his army. After having sacked the town
and liberated the Christian slaves, he restored

* Com grande batteria.

it to King Hassan, and, having returned to La
Goulette, which he fortified, he embarked with the
intention of taking the city of Africa.* He was prevented from doing so by contrary winds. Leaving
Calybia, which is also on the coast of Africa, he again
made sail, and landed for the first time in Sicily.
Having held an assembly there, and having given
suitable orders for the welfare of that kingdom, where
he left Don Ferdinand de Gonzaga as Viceroy, he
crossed the straits of Messina and proceeded to
Naples viâ Calabria. This was his third visit to
Italy. During this journey he had a fifth attack of
the gout at four different intervals. Whilst at
Naples the Emperor convoked an assembly, in which
he discussed the affairs of the kingdom. Here he
received news of the death of the Queen of England,
of the Prince of Piedmont, who was in Spain, and
of Francis Sforza, Duke of Milan.

Meantime Francis, King of France, commenced
a third war, with a view to seize the states of the
Duke of Savoy. This compelled His Imperial Majesty to leave Naples as soon as possible to take the
necessary measures to meet that invasion.

1536   The Emperor visited Rome, where he had his first
interview with His Holiness Pope Paul, as much
with a view to negotiate peace, for which propositions

---

* Mehedia — the ancient Aphrodisium.

had been made to him, as to induce him, should it
not be concluded, to take the part of the Duke of
Savoy, who, besides being a vassal of the empire, was
married to his sister-in-law and cousin-german, the
Infanta Doña Beatrice of Portugal. All these
matters were discussed at Rome, and led to various
negotiations, but did not end in anything.* A correspondence ensued, which the Emperor declined to
reply to, as beneath his notice.† He therefore
resolved to follow up his plans. Having made all
possible arrangements, and desirous of finding the
most suitable means to restore to the Duke of Savoy
the greater portion of his estates, of which he had
been forcibly despoiled, he left a portion of his
army near Turin and advanced another army through
the Netherlands, the command of which he intrusted
to the Count of Nassau, so as to alarm and do harm
to the enemy. Finally he accompanied the remainder of his troops, the command of which he
gave to Antonio de Leyva, and advanced as far as
Aix in Provence. This was the first time he entered
France with an army.‡ However, as the season was
far advanced, and it was necessary to oppose an
attack from the enemy, he withdrew with his whole

---

* Em Roma se trattou e praticou desta materia, e passaram muitas
cousas que não foram mais palvras sem effecto.

† Dónde se seguiram taes escritturas que Sua Majestade não quis
tomar cuidado de lhes respondèr, com a cousas muito frivolas.

‡ Que foi a primeira vez que entrou em França e com exercito.

army to Nice. From thence he proceeded to Genoa, where he dismissed and sent home all that portion of his army which was superfluous or useless. He took care to provide for the safety of the frontiers of Piedmont, of Montferrat, and of the state of Milan, of which he appointed the Marquis du Guast Governor and Captain-General. He then embarked at Genoa and returned to Barcelona. This was his fourth visit to Spain.

1537   The Emperor proceeded by post to Tordesillas, where the Queen his mother and the Empress his wife were residing. From thence he went to Valladolid, where he convoked the Cortes. For the sixth time he experienced a severe attack of the gout. He received the news that Duke Alexander de Medici had been treacherously killed, and he conferred the state of Florence upon Duke Cosmo de Medici. At this time the Infant don Louis of Portugal came to Valladolid to visit His Majesty and the Empress. It was the third visit which he paid to their Majesties. A few days afterwards the Emperor, leaving the Empress *enceinte*, proceeded to Monzon, where he convoked the ordinary Cortes. At this time the King of France, with troops hastily levied, invaded Flanders, and successively took Hesdin and Saint Pol, which latter town was soon recaptured by assault by an army assembled by the Queen of Hungary, commanded by General Count de Buren.

At the same time this army took Montreuil, and defeated Annibal, who was endeavouring to throw provisions into Terouane, then besieged. Nevertheless the city was relieved, the siege raised, and Montreuil abandoned.

The King of France, finding that the lands of the Duke of Savoy, which he had conquered in Piedmont, were wanting in provisions, and hard pressed by the Imperialists, and that, moreover, he had no means of coming to their support unless he could get rid of the resistance he encountered in Flanders, proposed a general armistice, which the Emperor had some difficulty in accepting, as he was aware of the sad condition of the territory which the King of France occupied in Piedmont. It resulted from these negotiations that the Emperor, having been informed of the sad condition of the said lands, and knowing that his forces were such as to render it impossible for them to receive succour, and from other reasons, concluded a general armistice with the said King, excepting only Piedmont. It happened, however, that the King of France sent so many men and troops into Piedmont that those lands were succoured.

The Cortes being closed, the Emperor returned by post to Valladolid to see the Empress, who had just been brought to bed of her fourth son, the Infant Don Juan, who died shortly afterwards. Almost at the same time died the Infanta Doña Beatrice of

Portugal, Duchess of Savoy. The Empress suffered much after her confinement, and since then until the day of her death was in very bad health. Whilst the Emperor was at Monzon negotiations for peace were opened between His Majesty and the King of France. The result was a conference between their respective ambassadors, which were, on the Emperor's side, Covos, Grand Commander of Léon, and M. de Granvelle, and on the King's side the Cardinal de Lorraine and the Constable of France; and as there were some hopes of an interview between their Majesties, the Emperor posted back to Barcelona to see what the negotiations had led to. However, Pope Paul observing that no conclusion had been come to, wished to interfere, offering to proceed in person to Nice, whilst the Emperor should go to Villafranca, and the King of France to Antibes; to which the Emperor agreed, because he was always inclined towards peace.*

Meantime the Emperor visited Perpignan and the frontier of Rousillon; on his return he found his brother-in-law, the Infant Don Louis of Portugal. This prince, from his good inclinations and a desire to work in the service of God and to do good,† had proceeded to Barcelona in all haste to see if he could be of any service in helping to the conclusion of

---

* Por ser sempre inclinado ao bem da paz.
† Pola boa inclinaciõ e desejos que tirha de se empregar em cousas do serviço de Deus e ser causa d'alguin bem.

peace. He was welcomed and entertained by His
Majesty in the most hospitable manner. But, considering that the journey to Nice had already been
agreed upon, and that His Holiness wished to act as
a mediator in this matter, His Majesty thought that
it was more advisable the Infant should not leave
Barcelona. He therefore returned. This was the
fourth visit to His Majesty.

As already stated, the Emperor had posted to
Barcelona; and there, conformable to his intention
of seeing what would ensue from these conferences,
he embarked for Nice. Whilst he was yet at Barcelona, negotiations for an armistice had been opened
between His Majesty and the King of France, and
the Emperor thought there was no inconvenience in
doing so, as he was going to Nice to treat for peace.
He therefore gave his assent on the point of embarking, and sent his ratification, although he had not yet
received that of the King, because he could not have
been informed of it in time. At the same time a
report was spread that a Turkish fleet was proceeding eastward, and with the purpose of preventing
this journey to Nice. His Majesty having arrived
at Pomègues,* near Marseilles, discerned some latine
sails coming eastwards. The Emperor, aware that
a short time previously the King of France had sent

1538

* In insulas quae sunt ante Assiliam, vulgo *Pomegas* dictas.
Sepulveda, xvii. 9.

some of his galleys in that direction, and fancying
that the vessels seen were of that number, made
the usual signals to them, so as to enter into con-
versation, and ascertain what news they had of
the Turkish fleet. But the said galleys either did
not or would not understand the signals; and
as they knew nothing of the armistice, and were
enemies, they opened fire upon the galleys of the
Emperor, and by hard rowing endeavoured to reach
the French coast. His Majesty, perceiving this,
ordered his galleys to give chase, and captured four
of them in the open sea; but he did not follow those
that had gained the land. The Emperor severely
reproached the captains of the galleys which he had
captured for the fault which they had committed, and
informed the Governor of Provence of this mistake,
and of the disorder which had ensued, making him
acquainted, moreover, with the armistice which
had been concluded at Barcelona, of which the
Governor had not received any intimation. Agreeable
to this truce, the Emperor restored the four captured galleys, and shortly afterwards he received the
ratification of the same by the King of France.

CHAPTER III.

Second Interview with the Pope.—Offensive League against the
Turks.—Interview between Charles and Francis I.—Charles
returns to Spain.—Convokes the Cortes at Toledo.—Capture of
Castel-Nuovo.—Death of the Empress (1539).—The Reformation.
—Appoints Prince Philip Governor of the Spanish dominions
during his absence.—Visits the King of France.—Visits Flanders.—
Count Egmont.—The Duchy of Gueldres.—The Duke of Clèves.—
M. de Granvelle.—The Queen of Hungary (1541).—Expedition to
Algeria.—The Spanish Fleet dispersed by a tempest.—Gives up
the Expedition.—Convokes the Cortes of Castille at Valladolid.—
Has a severe (the Ninth) Attack of Gout.—Holds the Cortes at
Monzon.—Renewal of War with France.—Pope Paul.—Diet at
Nüremberg.—Visits Italy again (1543).

THE Emperor continued his journey to Nice,
where he had a second interview with His Holiness, and, after having kissed his feet, he discussed
with him the different negotiations for peace with the
King of France, who had also arrived at Saint
Laurent. However, the conclusion of a truce was
all that was effected, and various motives led to it.*

The Emperor being at Villafranca, near Nice, and
desirous of seeing the most Christian Queen his sister,
as it was a long time since he had seen her, that
Princess, anxious to conciliate and comply with the

* Paras as quaes se averem de fazer ouve algúas razoes.

D 2

wishes of the Emperor her brother and of the King her husband, proceeded to Villafranca with Madame la Dauphine, the actual Queen,* Madame Margaret,† and many other ladies and high personages of France. As she found the time she spent with him extremely short, she returned a second time with a less numerous suite, and passed one night in the same city. The Queen having left, and the armistice having been concluded, the Emperor accompanied His Holiness as far as Genoa, where he experienced his seventh attack of the gout. This was his fifth visit to Italy. At this time the Pope, the Emperor, and the Signoria of Venice concluded an offensive league against the Turk; after which His Majesty embarked at Genoa to return to Spain.

As it had been agreed that an interview should take place between His Majesty and the King of France, His Majesty announced that on his return he should cruise along the French coast and stop at the port of Aigues-Mortes. The King at once, in a small boat, paid the Emperor a visit on board his galley, and the latter, in return for so great an act of courtesy, and to show equal confidence,‡ paid a visit to the King in the town of Aigues-Mortes. He

* Catherine of Medicis.
† Margaret, daughter of Francis I., afterwards Duchess of Savoy.
‡ Por pagar tão grande cortezia e mostrar a mesma confiança.

stopped there till the following day, well treated and feasted by the King, who, not satisfied with the courtesy he had already shown to the Emperor, insisted upon accompanying the Emperor in his gig, with his two sons, Monsieur le Dauphin and Monsieur d'Orléans, other princes of the blood, and high personages, to his galley. They all went on board, and great compliments were exchanged on all sides,[*] and various propositions were made, and the result was (as from the said visits and armistice) a great continuation of good friendship and greater confidence.[†] This was the second time that His Imperial Majesty saw the King of France, and the first time that he set foot in that kingdom as a friend. The Emperor again set sail, and returned for the fifth time to Spain. He landed at Barcelona and left for Valladolid, where he found the Empress much better than when he left her, but still indisposed. To put into execution the league which he had concluded, he for a second time convoked the general Cortes of all his kingdoms of Castille at Toledo, where their Majesties were residing, and where the support and assistance were discussed which it was possible and suitable to grant. In the same year a great dearth prevailed in Sicily. It was here principally that the fleet had to procure its provisions;

---

[*] Muitos comprimentos.
[†] Hua grande continuaçaõ de boa amizade e major confiança.

and, although the Emperor was quite prepared on his part, the Pope and the Venetians were of the opinion that it was not to be thought of to carry out this year the projected enterprise, and the contributions from the Cortes demanded by His Majesty were ceased to be levied. It however happened that His Holiness and the Signoria of Venice, deeming that it was not advisable to allow the year to pass by without doing something, united their fleets and sent them to oppose and fight the Turk by sea as well as by land. The result of this expedition was the capture of Castel-Nuovo.*

1539   The sufferings of the Empress continued, and her malady made daily progress, especially since it was ascertained that she was again *enceinte*: the Emperor remained the greater part of the year 1539 at Toledo. The state of the Empress grew worse, and having given birth to a fifth son it pleased God to call her unto himself, and it may be held for certain that he did so in his great mercy. This death caused great sorrow to everyone, especially to the Emperor, who ordered everything to be done that is customary and suitable under such circumstances.

Since the interview at Aigues-Mortes, negotiations had continued without interruption for the conclusion of a satisfactory and permanent peace between the

---

* Castel-Nuovo, in Dalmatia, at the Mouths of Cattaro.

Emperor and the King of France. As it happened that at this period certain innovations commenced to show themselves in Flanders, from which His Majesty had been absent since the year 1531, he deemed that his absence might be an obstacle to the remedy which those evils required, and give rise to other and still greater ones.* The Emperor had lost his companion; he was animated by a great desire to do everything that was possible to obtain a good result, and the conclusion of peace; and although he felt that the Prince his son was still much too young to govern in his absence and to replace the Empress in her functions, and despite the other inconveniences which were represented to him and brought to his notice, he hearkened only to the good and sincere intention he had to do good, and to fulfill his duties towards his subjects so as to prevent them suffering greater inconveniences and giving rise to more scandals.† He was also desirous of bringing to a conclusion certain matters which he had left in suspension in Germany. He had formed the design of embarking at Barcelona for Italy; but at the same time the King of France

---

* Naquelle tempo se commençaõ a mover algûas novitades nos estados de Flandres, e que estando sua Majestade Imperial ausente d'elles desdo anno de xxvi., sua longa absencia podia fazer falta para remedio dos males que havia e dar occasiáo a outros maiores.

† Pospondo tudo a bea e verdadeira intençao que tinha de bem fazer e comprir com o que devia a seus vasallos por evitar que não caissem em outros maiores inconvenientes e escandalos.

sent him many pressing invitations to visit his kingdom, offering all security and a hearty welcome, whilst
on the contrary he would have been much grieved
had His Majesty shown any mistrust or acted otherwise.* The Emperor therefore decided on taking
his departure from Spain, leaving for the first time
the government of his kingdoms to the Prince his
son, despite his youth.

At the end of this year the Emperor put this resolution into execution, and, on the word and the
promise of the King of France (with whom a truce
had been concluded at Villafranca, near Nice), he
passed through his kingdom, where His Majesty was
fêted and well received. This was the third interview
between their Majesties, the third time that His
Majesty set foot in France, and the second time that
he entered the kingdom as a friend.

1540　　The Emperor visited Flanders for the fourth time.
Here he took the most prompt measures possible to
put a stop to the disorders which had sprung up
there.†

He commenced the fortress of Ghent, assembled
the estates, and visited the greater portion of the
domains. During this visit he experienced at the

* Offerecendo lhe toda segurança e bom trattamento e que do
contrario receperia grande pezar e sentimento polas monstras que
Sua Majestade daria de desconfiança.

† Proveo ó remedio ó mais prestes que pode as desordés que
havia.

Hague, in Holland, an eighth attack of gout, and conformably to the intention he entertained, and to the desire which had always animated him to conclude a good peace, he offered to the King of France, immediately he had arrived in the said states, such favourable conditions, that he was surprised to find they were not accepted and the desired peace not concluded.*

Some time previously Count Charles of Egmont had died, after having for many years ruled the duchy of Gueldres, which, however, did not belong to him. More than that, he had seized upon every opportunity to develope and increase his power, and at various periods he had attempted to get possession of Friesland, Overyssel, and Gröningen, from which he was always driven back by the Imperialists, and which territories were in the peaceful possession of His Majesty. Not content with this, he made war against the Bishop of Utrecht, who was a prince of the empire, and took the town of Utrecht from him by force. As soon as the Emperor heard of this, to whom the Bishop had sued for assistance (an obligation to which he was bound as lord of the fief), and it was all the stronger, as it was necessary to maintain tranquillity in the Netherlands,† he concerted measures with the

* Offerecendo lhe tao grandes partidos que se maravilhou de não serem d'elle acceitados e de se não seguir a paz desejada.

† Nos Payses-Baixos de haver quietação.

Bishop, and came to his assistance in such guise that the said Count Charles of Egmont was driven out of Utrecht by the Imperial troops. The Emperor, who proceeded there in person shortly afterwards, ordered a new fortress to be constructed there, and for this purpose obtained from the Pope and from the empire all the necessary acts and ratifications.

After the death of Charles of Egmont, Duke William of Clèves seized upon the government of the duchy of Gueldres, asserting a claim to it. His Imperial Majesty, seeing how matters stood, and how he consequently ought to and could act, made him offers, the conditions of which were such that they ought reasonably to have been accepted. But, at the request, and through the intrigues of France (the French were dissatisfied, although without grounds, with the terms of the peace, which were not conformable to their wishes and designs),* the Duke, who moreover was young and followed the counsel of his mother, would not accept them. The Emperor having thus achieved all that was to be done in the states of Flanders, and having convoked a Diet at Ratisbon, where he wished distinctly to show his claims relative to the duchy of Gueldres, resolved to leave for the said Diet, as already, whilst in Spain, he had opened

* Como por os Francerez ficarem discontentos (ainda que sem razão) das condiçoês da paz por não serem todas conformees a sua vontade e ao que tinham proposto.

negotiations on the subject with the states of the empire. The King of the Romans came to visit his brother in Flanders, and the deputies of the empire assembled at Worms to deliberate upon this question. The Emperor, finding that all was not quite settled in the Netherlands, requested the King his brother to remain there during his absence, and he also charged M. de Granvelle and his other ministers to push on matters whilst he was attending the said Diet. However, as this assembly at Worms, and the negotiations which took place, did not lead to the result which he had anticipated, everything was reserved for the future Diet of Ratisbon.

The Emperor, leaving for the second time the 1541 government of the Netherlands to the care of the Queen of Hungary, proceeded to the Diet at Ratisbon, for the first time passing through the state of Luxembourg. This was the Emperor's fourth visit to Germany. He had convoked this Diet chiefly to establish concord and to effect a remedy in the state of religious affairs. After various debates, the Emperor observed that the princes of the empire had not attended this Diet, and that they were still far from a conclusion, and still more so from the means of execution which ought to be adopted;* moreover, the report was current that

* Que avia pouco de conclusaõ e menos d'execuçaõ que convinha fazer.

the Turk intended to invade Austria, and no order
had been given to oppose that invasion and to take
the necessary measures of defence. Already, before
this news was received, the Emperor, from various
reasons which actuated him, had on his return to
Spain made great naval preparations for an expedition to Algeria. He therefore left Ratisbon before he
was fully informed of the invasion of the Turk, and
started for Italy to embark, and commence the said
enterprise. This was His Majesty's sixth visit there.
Immediately on his arrival, positive news was received that the Turk was making great preparations
to invade Hungary. From this reason the Emperor
proceeded to Lucca, where he had his third interview with Pope Paul to arrange the means for
organising a defence against the Turk. But finding
that this interview and these negotiations led to no
result, he proceeded to Spezzia, a port in the Gulf
of Genoa, to wait there until his fleet was in perfect
readiness. Already the equipment and preparations
for this fleet had occupied more time than was necessary; and although the season was almost past, nevertheless, as the outlays incurred could not be turned
to any other account, and from other reasons which,
as already said, actuated the Emperor, considering
that weather is in the hands of God,* he embarked
at the said port of Spezzia for Corsica, which he saw

---

* Considerando que o tempo estava em mão de Deus.

for the first time, and from thence for Algiers,
touching at the island of Sardinia, at Majorca, and
at Minorca, for the second time. This was the
eighth time that he crossed the Mediterranean, and
the second time that he landed in Africa. During
this journey the weather was seasonable. The
Spanish fleet also arrived, and after a few skirmishes,
when the troops were already suitably posted to
attack the town, and provided with everything that
was necessary to open their batteries, so fierce a
tempest arose on sea that many vessels perished,
and the army on land also suffered considerably.

Nevertheless the men mutually assisted each
other, and the best order possible was organised, as
well to resist the fury of the sea as the attacks of the
enemy by land. Finally the annoyances became so
great that the Emperor deemed it the wisest plan to
relinquish the expedition and put to sea. But this
could not be done immediately, as the tempest had
not subsided. He was therefore obliged to march
twenty miles by land, to cross two large rivers, so as
to reach Cape Matafous, where he reembarked.

The whole time the army was on land (it remained
there twelve days before reembarking) it suffered
from great want of provisions, because, as already
said, the weather was so boisterous that nothing
could be got from the ships. After those twelve
days the Emperor set sail during a great storm, and

was compelled to touch at Bougie. The winds were
so contrary, and he was retained so long, that he and
his troops suffered much from the scarcity of provisions; and the evils would have been still greater
had the fine weather not returned. The tempest was
so fierce that everyone sought shelter where best he
could, and many ships were driven in directions
quite contrary to where they wished to go. Nevertheless the troops recovered so well that, without so
much loss as might have been expected from such
weather, they all returned to the appointed rendez-
vous. The Emperor dismissed the superfluous men
and those least wanted, and the others returned to
their garrisons. The Emperor, having embarked at
Bougie, arrived with fair weather at Majorca for the
third time, from whence Prince Doria returned to
Genoa with his galleys, after passing by Barcelona.

1542   The Emperor, with the Spanish galleys, touched for
the first time at Ivica; for the ninth time he navi-
gated the Mediterranean. He arrived at Carthagena:
this was his sixth visit to Spain. He then continued
his route as far as Ocaña, where he met his children,
the Prince of Spain and the Infantas.

In the commencement of the year 1542, the
Emperor proceeded to Valladolid, to hold the Cortes
of the kingdom of Castille. Here he experienced a
ninth attack of gout, and at the monastery of La
Mejorada he suffered from it generally in nearly all

his limbs. At this time negotiations were on foot
for the marriage of the Prince his son with the
Infanta Doña Maria of Portugal, and of Prince Juan
of Portugal with the Infanta Doña Juana, second
daughter of His Majesty.

As soon as the Cortes had terminated, the Emperor,
although unwell, proceeded as quickly as he could,
passing through Navarre, to hold the Cortes of the three
kingdoms of Aragon at Monzon, with the intention of
returning as soon as possible to Germany to provide
some remedy for the affairs of religion, and to recover
by all means in his power the duchy of Gueldres,
which belonged to him. The King of France, however, seeing the bad success which had attended the
Emperor in his enterprise against Algiers, and fancying that the outlays he had been put to must have
drained his finances, commenced by making a small
complaint, and the Emperor replied to him by offering
all the justifications to which he was bound by the
conditions of the truce concluded at Nice.* The
King of France nevertheless transmitted to him from
all parts the assurance that he had not the slightest
intention of going to war with him ;† but he suddenly
attacked the Emperor in the Netherlands, Martin

* Algûa fraca queixa a qual se tinham offerecido todas as justi-
ficações que o Emperador polas condiçoes da tregoa feita em Niza
estava obrigado.
† Assegurando o de todas as partes que não tinha intento de lhe
fazer guerra algûa.

Van Rossem commencing operations in Gueldres, M. d'Orleans in Luxembourg, and M. de Vendôme in the states of Flanders and in Artois. Moreover, he ordered his son the Dauphin to lay siege to Perpignan, and proceeded himself as far as Narbonne to stimulate the enterprise. Nevertheless, by the grace of God, the Emperor, and those who had the management of his affairs, set things so well in order, and organised so able a defence, that this time the said King did nothing of importance.

At this period Pope Paul, not satisfied with having issued a bull, which was a testimony of his good will, but which had scarcely any other effect, convoked a general Council at Trent, and at the same time sent his Legates to His Majesty and to the King of France, not only to invite them and to exhort them to peace, but also to restrain them by ecclesiastical censure if they would not obey his behest to conclude a truce. This happened, as already said, at the period His Majesty was attacked, and when the French were repulsed on all sides and compelled to withdraw. His Imperial Majesty, seeing with what intentions His Holiness wished to effect a peace between their Majesties, and that thereby His Imperial Majesty would have been mulcted and dispossessed of all that had been taken from him by a sudden and unexpected invasion, did not think it either equitable or suitable to accept such propositions of peace; but he felt indignant, and obliged to reconquer what belonged to him, and to show his resentment for such an injury. The Emperor therefore rejected the said propositions, and would not hearken to them at all.* He somewhat drily dismissed the Legate, who had addressed him in a tone without that respect which was due to His Majesty.† Hè however still protested that he was, as he always had been, inclined to treat for peace, provided that the adverse party was governed by reason, and provided that the peace was sure and suitable to the service of God and to the welfare of Christianity.‡

The Cortes of Aragon having terminated, the Emperor left for Barcelona. He had sent the Prince his son from Monzon to Saragossa, that he should be recognised Prince of that kingdom; from thence His Majesty proceeded with him to Barcelona, where he was

---

* Vendo Sua Magestade Imperial a tençáõ, com que Sua Santitade queria trattar de por em paz Suas Magestades, pela qual Sua Magestade Imperial ficara aggravado, e desapossado do que per aquella subita e repentina invasáõ lhe fora tomado, não lhe parecendo nem justo, nem conveniente acceitar taes modos e meios de paz, antes sentindo se mais stimulado e forçado a recobrar o seu e mostrar o sentimento, que tinha de hum tal aggravo, refusou os dittos modos propostos e de nenhua maneira os quis ouvir.

† Despedio assaz seccamente ao legado o qual tambem tinha usado de termos pouco graves, nem guardava o respeito que a Sua Magestade se devia.

‡ Offerecendo se com tudo de estar, como sempre esteve, prestes para trattar da paz, com tanto que a parte contraria se accommoda sea razáo, e ella fosse segura e conveniente ao serviço de Deus e bem da Christandade.

E

also recognised. Having passed through Valencia,
where the same ceremonial was observed, the Emperor
took the direction of Alcala to see his daughters. Here
the affiance *per verba de futuro* of his daughter
the Infanta Doña Juana took place with Prince Don
Juan of Portugal, according to what had been agreed
upon. This done, the Emperor proceeded to Madrid,
which city he left as soon as he could, because he
much desired, according to his first intention, to
return to Germany. In fact he had convoked a Diet
at Nüremberg, to discuss defensive measures against
the Turk, and matters of religion. The King his
brother and M. de Granvelle proceeded there, in the
name of His Majesty, with many others of his
ministers whom he had sent there. The Emperor,
having terminated all that he had to do in the
kingdoms of Spain, commenced his journey, having
left for the second time during his absence the
Prince, his son, Governor of the said kingdoms. He
therefore left Madrid, and arrived at Barcelona,
which city he would willingly have left earlier, but
1543 various obstacles prevented his embarking before
May 1, and in consequence of storms and boisterous weather he was not able to gain the open sea
till the 19th of that month, when the weather
was still unsettled and doubtful. When off Pomègues, near Marseilles, some French galleys sallied
out and commenced skirmishing, supported by the

land batteries; but they were so ably responded to that they were compelled to retreat, and place themselves under the protection of the artillery on shore. The Emperor, not wishing any delay, continued his journey to Genoa. This was the tenth time he crossed the Mediterranean, and the seventh time he landed in Italy.

CHAPTER IV.

WHILST passing in front of Nice the Emperor
learnt that the galleys of France wished to
capture the castle of that town, and whilst His
Majesty was landing at Genoa Prince Doria approached with his galleys to watch the movements
of those of France. Observing that they came with
the intention of executing the project attributed to
them, he attacked them so briskly that he captured
four of them. At this period His Majesty learnt
that Barbarossa was expected with a large fleet to
support the King of France.

This Barbarossa arrived later, remained at Toulon
during the whole time the war against the Emperor
lasted, and returned without having performed any
act of importance. His Majesty proceeded to
Busseto, where he was joined by His Holiness, as
much to discuss the affairs of Germany as to see if

there were no possible means of concluding a peace.*
This was the Emperor's fourth interview with Pope
Paul, and he experienced a tenth attack of gout. A
few days afterwards, perceiving how little good resulted from this interview, he continued † his journey
towards Germany, where he found himself for the
fifth time.

As the Diet had not been long sitting, and the
Emperor, in a time so replete with troubles, did not
see any chance of regulating and discussing the
affairs of religion, he continued his journey as far as
Spires, where he made all the necessary preparations
to enter the campaign with a good army, at the
head of which he placed Don Ferdinand de Gonzaga. He was desirous of resenting the injuries and
damage perpetrated by the King of France, who
had penetrated into the territory of Hainault as far
as Binche, and had taken Landrecies, which he was
fortifying. He was also compelled to do so by the
war waged against him by Duke William of Clèves,
who had taken up arms at the instigation of the King
of France, and in concert with him. On his way, the
Emperor heard of the defeat and route of the Duke's
troops at Heinsberg. Nevertheless His Majesty, on his

---

* Para se verem ambos assi polas cousas d'Alemanha, como por
ver se haveria algúne modo de paz.

† Poucos dios despois vendo o pouco effeito, que daquella vista
resultava.

arrival at Spires, wished, the better to justify himself, to propose to the electors, who had assembled on
the banks of the Rhine, to treat with the said Duke
of Clèves by means of a pacific arrangement as
regarded the duchy of Gueldres. This proposal did
not meet with a good reception, and the only plan
left for him was to reassemble his army and advance with it (this was the sixth time he was on the
Rhine) as far as Bonn, from whence he took the
direction of Duren. Having there made a reconnaissance of the ground, he established his batteries,
bombarded the town, and carried it by storm. The
Prince of Orange then came up with his army from
the Netherlands. The two armies having united,
and Duren having been captured, as already stated,
with other possessions and lands appertaining to the
duchy of Gueldres, as also to the duchy of Clèves and
of Juliers, His Majesty took the direction of Rure-
mond, which immediately surrendered, and from
thence he advanced in the direction of Venloo.
And as Duke Henri of Brunswick arrived as a
friend of the said Duke of Clèves, the Emperor
demonstrated and exposed to him his error, ex-
horting him to renounce it. At this time the mother
of the Duke of Clèves died. This latter recognised the bad counsel he had received, and the wisest
men of the states of Gueldres also entreated him to
withdraw from the danger he was in, and to follow

better advice; he did so, and came and threw himself at the feet of His Majesty, confessing his fault and asking pardon. He handed over and restored the whole state of Gueldres to the Emperor. But the Emperor, considering that the error of the Duke originated rather in his youth than from any evil inclination or wish to do evil, ordered the towns and localities taken from him in other territories to be restored to him. Not content with what he had done, and seeing the Duke's repentance, and how well he persevered in his good intentions, he took his marriage into hand; in fact he gave him in marriage his niece, a daughter of the King of the Romans. This marriage increased the obligations of the said Duke towards His Majesty, and the love of His Majesty for that Prince. At the commencement of the spring the King of France, to be the first in the field, and to be enabled to oppose superior forces to the Emperor, brought forth two armies destined to wage war in the Netherlands. A portion of one of these armies, in which the King was present in person, occupied Landrecies, and the other portion established itself in the neighbourhood whilst the fortifications were strengthened. The two sons of the King had meantime marched on Binche, from whence they were driven back with loss, without having accomplished anything. Finally, M. d'Orleans joined the other army, which was at

Luxembourg. This town, not being in a state of
defence, had surrendered, and had been fortified
by the French. At the same time happened what
has already been related before of the war that
the Duke of Clèves, at the instigation of the same
King, had commenced in Brabant. The Emperor,
having put an end to that war of Clèves, and having
taken possession of Gueldres, as already stated, left,
suffering from the gout, Venloo for Diest, where the
Estates of the Netherlands were assembled. They
granted him a large subsidy, on the footing of the
one granted to him the preceding year. This was
the fifth visit of His Majesty to the Netherlands.
The King of France, apprised of all these facts,
withdrew with his troops into his kingdom, after
having fortified Landrecies.

This done, the Emperor, leaving under the walls of
Landrecies the army which was in the Netherlands,
with the gendarmerie which the King of England
had sent to him in virtue of conventions which had
been concluded, ordered the army which he had with
him to march, as also that which had arrived from
England, as far as Guise. But as the season was
already advanced, and the weather inclement, he
soon ordered it back to join that before Landrecies.
The Emperor, although suffering much from the
gout, left Diest to attend the siege; and knowing that
the King of France was assembling new troops to

relieve the besieged, he did not wish to be absent from his armies. He therefore established his quarters at Avesnes, although, as already stated, suffering from the gout, and he remained there until the troops sent to the succour of the garrison of Landrecies had withdrawn. This was his tenth attack of the gout.

The King of France, knowing that his troops were in danger and in want of provisions, proceeded with his army to Chateau-Cambrésis, from whence he sent a heavy body of cavalry to reconnoitre the ground, so as to attempt to succour the garrison of Landrecies. To prevent this the armies of the Emperor formed a junction, and made such a resistance that this cavalry did not attain its object and had little subject of congratulation.* It is true that during this time some French knights, with sacks of gunpowder and a small supply of provisions, of which the besieged stood much in need, succeeded in entering Landrecies at a point where there was no obstacle, which rallied the besieged a little. As the season was advanced and the weather bad, and as, moreover, the chief object of the Emperor, when he ordered his army in France to besiege Landrecies, was to compel the King to give battle,† he ordered his army to decamp, and approached France.

---

* Nem tene muito de que se jactar.
† Forçar el rey de França a lhe dar batalha.

On the same day the Emperor, still unwell and
carried in a litter, left Avesnes and passed the night
at Quesney. From thence he rejoined his army,
which had already taken up a position opposite that
of the King of France. On the following morning
His Majesty, leaving his quarters, advanced with all
his men within cannon range of the enemy, close to
the King's camp, and offered him battle. A few
skirmishes and discharges of artillery took place on
both sides, and finally a bold charge against the
French, who had the worst of it, and they thought it
advisable not again to leave their entrenchments. The
Emperor, finding they would not come out, advanced
with his army close up to the enemy's camp. The
following day was passed in skirmishing : at night-fall
the King withdrew with his army, and retreated as
far as Guise. The Emperor, through the negligence
of his scouts, was ignorant of this retreat until the
following day; the result was that he could not
come up with the King and his army.* He advanced as far as a wood or thicket, to a distance of

---

* Movendo ao outro dia pela manhãa, Sua Magestade do ditto
alojamento se foi por com toda sua gente a tiro de bombarda, junto
ao arraial del Rey e lhe apresentou batalha. E com algúas escaramuças e tiros d'artilheria de hua e outra parte e com hua bon
carga, que se deu aos Franceses daqual elles ficarem com o peor, se
contentaram por entonces e tinerao por bem não sair do arraial. E
vendo o Emperador que elles não fariam outra cousa, se foi por com
sua gente bem junto ao campo enemigo; o outro dia se passou com
algúas escaramuças, e vindo a noute el Rey com seu exercito se

three leagues, but he could not, owing to the disorder of his matchlock-men (who most of them were
followed or accompanied by more baggage than
soldiers ought to have), attempt to cross the wood
with his army. A few light cavalry and matchlock-
men, and a disorderly few, traversed the thicket.
M. le Dauphin observed it, and having collected his
French gendarmes he turned round and charged his
pursuers. The latter sought refuge in the thicket,
and then returned to the infantry. It may easily be
believed that, if the Emperor had had his matchlock-
men, with whom he coûld have passed through the
thicket in safety, he might have attained in part the
object of his desires; * but as nothing else was to be
done on this day, and as it was already late, he left
the thicket, and established his quarters in the very
camp and on the very spot which the King of
France had left. He arrived there at one hour after
midnight.

The Emperor remained some days at Chateau-Cambrésis, to see if he could not undertake something
against his enemy. But the latter resolved to disband his army at once, and sent the troops back to
their garrisons. The Emperor, considering also that

---

partio, e se foi tee Guisa. E não sabendo o Emperador por des-
cuido dos seus desta partida atee a outro dia pela manhãa, foi no
alcânce del Rey com sua gente.

* Chegara em parte ao fim do seus desejos.

the festival of All Saints had already passed, determined to do likewise; and consequently he proceeded
to Cambray, and from thence to Brussels, where he
was taken ill (not from the gout) and was laid up
during the rest of the year. At the end of this same
year the Princess of Spain, the Infanta Doña Maria
of Portugal, was, conformably to the engagements
which had been made, taken to Castille and handed
over to the Prince of Spain at Salamanca, where
their nuptials were solemnised, after having been
contracted *per verba de presenti.*

1544　The Emperor, leaving the Queen of Hungary his
sister, for the third time, Governor of the Netherlands, left Brussels, and for the sixth time went up
the Rhine as far as Spires. This was also the sixth
time that he entered Germany, where he had convoked a Diet with a view to explain to the electors of
the empire the causes which had induced him to
undertake the Gueldres expedition and to march
against the King of France, causes which have been
briefly given above, but which were more developed
in the proposition then made. And seeing that at
this moment there did not appear any likelihood of
the Turk advancing against Christendom, and that it
was also impossible to do anything in matters of
religion,* or to discuss any important affairs, he
demanded a subsidy against the King of France, who

* E tambem que a cerca da religião não se podia fazer.

had seized upon various towns and lands of the empire, and who daily accomplished or negotiated things to its great detriment.* This having been well considered and fully appreciated, all granted good aid to His Imperial Majesty.

Whilst the Emperor was on his way to Spires, Pope Paul sent Cardinal Farnese to His Majesty, under colour and pretext of making representations to him, and of endeavouring to treat for peace. The Emperor, well aware that these were empty words and sheer pretexts, would not allow himself to be caught, nor relinquish the plans and pursuit of the enterprise which he had commenced to recover the territory of which he had been despoiled. Thus he soon dismissed the said Cardinal, declaring that he was always willing to negotiate for a sincere, good, and permanent peace.† Then, supported and strengthened by the aid he had received from the empire, he commenced reassembling his army.

---

* Contra el Rey de França o qual tinha tomado algúas Cidades e terras do Imperio, e fazia e trattava cada dia cousas em grande detrimento.

† Indo o Emperador por caminho para Espira, veo ter com sua Magestade o Cardinal Farnea da parte do Papa Paulo sob color e sombra di amoestar e querrer trattar de paz. E conhecendo Sua Magestade que nisto não havia mais que palavras sem algúa mostra de boa conclusão, não se quis deixar levar d'ellos, nem d'executar a intenção, e seguir a boa causa, que tinha e a impresa começada, por recobrar o que lhe fora tomado. E assi dispedio logo ao ditto Cardeal, offerecendo se de estar sempre prestes para entender e trattar de hua verdedeira, boa, segura e firma paz.

Meantime the Emperor received the news that
the army which he had in Italy had been defeated
near Carignano. It was at a bad time, and under
bad circumstances.* Whatever might come of it,
having previously learnt that the city of Luxembourg,
although carefully fortified, was short of provisions,
and that the King of France was endeavouring to
throw supplies into it, he ordered, in all haste, Don
Ferdinand de Gonzaga, to whom he had entrusted
the command of his army, to prevent any supplies
reaching that city. This General, with a small body
of men, performed his mission so well that the city
shortly surrendered.

The Emperor soon reinforced his army in such
guise that his said Captain-General captured in a
few days many towns and strongholds on the French
frontier on the Lorraine side, and laid siege to Saint
Dizier. On his part, the Emperor left Spires and
passed through Metz, to join him with the remainder
of the army. This was the fourth time that His
Majesty entered France, and the second time as an
enemy. Fire was opened against Saint Dizier, the
assault given, and the town captured in a few days.
At this siege, the Prince of Orange was struck by a
cannon-ball in the trenches, and died shortly afterwards.

According to what had been agreed upon between

* Que foi em mao tempo e occasião.

His Majesty and the King of England, the said King had come in person with a large army to molest and attack the kingdom of France,* and His Majesty had also sent to him the forces he had promised by the said convention, under the orders of M. de Buren. The said King had stopped at the siege of Boulogne and of Montreuil; and during the long lapse of time during which His Majesty was before Saint Dizier, the King of France had leisure to assemble his whole army, and to garrison the greater portion of the frontiers of his kingdom. The Emperor, taking all this into consideration, observing moreover that he had not at his command as sufficient a supply of provisions as he required, and that the season was far advanced, found difficulties for any ulterior enterprise.

However, not to leave the King of England alone against his enemy, he would not retire with his army. Already previously, during the siege of Saint Dizier, he had captured Vitry, defeated the French light cavalry there, and made other incursions. The Emperor, leaving the town of Saint Dizier and other more important places in a good state of defence, and persevering in the intention already mentioned above of employing every means to bring the King of France to give battle,† resolved to penetrate into

---

* Molestar e offender o reino de França.

† De por todos modos e meios tirar e trazer el rhe de França a lhe dar batalha.

the interior of that kingdom as far as he could, always seeking the said King and his army.* Consequently, the Emperor, passing by Vitry, established himself in a plain near Châlons. Here some good skirmishes took place, where the French gained nothing, and where they had no reason to be satisfied with the pistols and small matchlocks of the German horsemen.† But as Châlons had a strong garrison, and there was a French army at three short leagues from it on the other side of the Marne, considering, moreover, that the Emperor and his army had no other provisions to depend upon except what they found in the country villages and small towns, it appeared to His Majesty that he ought not to make a longer stay in this locality.‡ And although he had marched during the whole of the day upon which he arrived there, he left with his whole army at ten o'clock in the evening; and so quick was the advance, that at daybreak he found himself in view and in face of the spot where the French had taken position with their entrenchments, carefully fortified, especially on the side on which the Emperor had arrived.

---

* Determinou d'entrar o mais que pudesse por dentro daquello reino, indo se sempre inegando e buscando ao ditto Rey e seu exercito.

† Nem ficaram muito contentes dos pistoletes ou pinquenos arcabuzes dos Alemaes de cavallo.

‡ A Sua Magestade pareceo que nao convenha fazer mais longa demora no quelle lugar.

The Marne flowed between the two armies. His Majesty might certainly have crossed the Marne, as there was a wooden bridge, which, although broken down, might have been repaired so as to allow the passage of the infantry. There was also one where both cavalry and infantry might cross. But when that was accomplished, there would still have been much to be done, to the great disadvantage of the Emperor's troops. For supposing the bridge and ford crossed (which could only be done in file), it would have been necessary to reform in order, as a fine open plain lay in front which could be swept by the enemy's artillery. It would have then been necessary to advance to the attack under continual fire; and when all this was done there was still a branch of the Marne, which, though narrow, was deep, and offered some difficult points which could not be overcome without disorder. Then it was necessary to climb a hill or mound to reach the enemy, who counted a good number of Swiss in his ranks. The Emperor saw that all these difficulties rendered it impossible to put the army in good order of battle; he therefore persisted in the resolution which he had taken to make a long march that day to get ahead of the French army. In fact it was the Emperor's intention to advance, so as to find the places he passed through undefended, and he hoped that he should force the French to advance so far as to offer him the opportunity he

F

desired. On the same morning Count William of
Fürstenberg, not knowing what he was about,*
crossed the above-mentioned ford, and fell into the
hands of the French. On the other hand, Prince
de la Roche-sur-Yon, whilst endeavouring to join the
French camp with his company, came across some
Imperial light horse, who pursued him and charged
in such guise that he, his lieutenant, and many others
were made prisoners and his men put to flight.

On the same day, the Emperor continued to
advance, and almost reached Ay, where he was
stopped by the bad state of the road and the numerous streams. Moreover, his rear-guard did not
arrive till ten in the evening. Thus the army had
been marching for twenty-four hours, and on the preceding day it had performed the same march. If it
is permitted to form a judgement on what might
have happened if the Emperor had that day reached
Epernay, which was only a short French league
farther on (the thing was impossible), so as to
have enabled the army to cross the river on the
morrow over the stone bridge of that city, and by
the boats constructed on the same river, he might
have, by following the ridge of hill above mentioned, attacked the French camp by the slopes,
which had not yet been fortified, and God would

---

* Não sabendo o que fazia.

have given the victory to whom it pleased Him.[*]
However, in consequence of the obstacles already
mentioned, the Emperor did not reach Epernay till
the evening of the following day, and he proposed in
council what has been related above. But this project could not be carried out, because, in consequence
of the delay of this day which had been lost, the
French had time to fortify all the slopes as they had
done on the other side; of which fact the Emperor received speedy information. In consequence the Emperor left Epernay, advancing always with great dili-
gence and precaution.[†] But the road offered great
obstructions, owing to the numerous streams and
rivulets that intersected them. In some localities
they were so bad that it was often necessary to
make long detours, so that, when it was hoped to get
over two or three French leagues during the day, it
happened that, owing to the circuitous road taken,
not more than one was accomplished. This decided the Emperor to send forward in advance a
good number of men without their baggage, that
they might capture (and they did capture it) the
town of Chateau-Thierry. The Emperor followed
them as fast as he could, always with the intention
of advancing farther and continuing his route.

[*] E Deus dera a victoria a quem fora servido.
[†] Com granda pressa e cuidado.

CHAPTER V.

Negotiations for Peace, continued.—Charles consults the King of
England.—Mission of the Bishop of Arras.—Surrender of Boulogne
to the King of England.—Surrender of Soissons to Charles.—
Henry consents to Peace.—Conclusion of Peace.—M. d' Orleans
and M. de Vendôme visit the Emperor.—Charles disbands his
Army.—Is laid up with Gout at Ghent.—Convocation of the
Council of Trent.—The Diet of Worms.—Secret Treaty against
the Protestants.—The Pope's Legate is alarmed.—He refuses to
join the Treaty without seeing the Pope. — The Pope convokes a
Consistory and preaches a Crusade against the Protestants.—
Death of the Duke of Orleans.

NOW it must be known that, during this expedition of the Emperor into France, the King's
ministers never ceased to negotiate daily, and to offer
proposals for peace; and the Emperor, who was, and
always had been, desirous of peace,* had not rejected them. If at the outset the King's ministers
had spoken of peace, they did so much more eagerly
when they saw that His Majesty had passed Châlons
with his whole army.† They therefore continued

---

* Aoque Sua Magestade como quem lhe era e fora sempre tao
affeiçoado.
† E so de principio elles trattavam e pratticavam de paz, muito
mais e com maior istancia o fizeram, quando viram Sua Magestade
passar de Chalon com seu exercito e tanto se continuaram, e tao
grande calor se deu a estas prattieas de paz, que vieram quasi a con-
cordar nos artigos et condiçoes della.

these negotiations, and displayed such zeal that the
articles and conditions of peace had almost been
settled. Nevertheless, as the King of England was
before Boulogne, as already stated, and as His
Majesty, who had advanced so far into the interior
of France, had no news of what he was doing, and
had no means of sending him any information as
regards his own acts, he could not, according to the
conventions concluded with the said King, sign a
peace with the King of France without the know-
ledge and the consent of the King of England. To
effect this, the ministers of the King of France
allowed the Bishop of Arras, the Emperor's minister,
to proceed, on the part of His Majesty, to inform
the King of England of what was actually taking
place. The Emperor informed him that if with his
forces he would on his side penetrate farther into
France, he was ready on his part to push forward
his advance and his enterprise until the two armies
should form their junction before Paris, or in any
locality deemed most suitable.* Should he not
accept this proposal, he asked his consent that His
Majesty might negotiate for peace, including him
according to what had been agreed upon before-
hand.

* Offerecendo che que se com suas forças e gente queria da sua
parte entrar mais per França, que o Emperador da sua continuaria
seu caminho e empresa atee se arrem ajuntar os dous exercitos la
para a parte de Paris, ou aonde melhor parecesse.

However, during this time the King of England, continuing the siege of Boulogne, pressed the place so hard that it was compelled to surrender, which naturally gave him great satisfaction.* Finding the season far advanced, and considering the great outlays this war had cost him, he came to the conclusion that he had neither the necessary means nor resources to advance farther into France,† and consented that the Emperor should conclude peace.

Now, whilst the Emperor was awaiting, as already stated, a prompt reply from the King of England, he found that he could not remain longer in the locality where he was, owing to the want of all necessary things, experienced by his army, and he also found that it would be difficult for him to continue to advance. In fact, from the motives indicated higher up, he could not have been more rapid in his movements; and the hostile army being unfettered in its action, owing to the river which separated it from the Emperor, had time to gain the advance and organise its forces. The result was that the Emperor, in want of provisions, which it was impossible for him to procure so far in the interior of France (from Chateau-Thierry to Paris there are scarcely

* Doque elle, e com justa cousa, estava mui contente.

† E vendo a sazaõ ir declinando muito, e os grandes gastos uq fizera nesta guerra, nem ter as commodidades e apercebimentos necessarios para poder entrar mais per França.

twenty short leagues), could not remain long enough
to attack those places which would have defended
themselves—a point of the highest importance.* The
Emperor weighed all these considerations, the more
so as the soldiers' pay was in arrear, and the money
requisite to pay them was to be had in the Netherlands; but there was no means of conveying it, and
his determination was almost imposed upon him by
necessity, as well to obtain sooner the reply of the
King of England as to approach the Netherlands,
where he could more easily procure money and
other indispensable things, and also to organise his
plans better, according to the reply he should receive
from the King of England. He therefore left
Chateau-Thierry, taking the road to Soissons, which
surrendered on his approach. From this place he
could carry out the propositions which he had made
to the King of England, as well and even better
than he could have done at Chateau-Thierry.

Meantime the reply of the King of England
arrived. As already said, he consented that the
Emperor should conclude peace. Peace having been
concluded, M. d'Orleans arrived on a visit to the
Emperor. M. de Vendôme also arrived soon afterwards, and the Emperor continued his journey with
his whole army as far as Cateau-Cambrésis, where

* Cousa que fora da grande importancia.

he paid it off and dismissed it, and from thence
he proceeded to Cambray, where he found his sister
the Queen of Hungary, as also the hostages that
were to be handed over to him. With all this company he returned to Brussels. This was the sixth
time that he revisited his states of Flanders. Shortly
afterwards he received there Her Most Christian
Majesty and M. d'Orleans, accompanied by many
lords and ladies, who had left after having been
hospitably entertained for some days. The Emperor turned his attention to the affairs of his states
of Flanders with the intention of visiting them.
He therefore left Brussels, where he had been
threatened with an attack of the gout, for Ghent.
In this city he experienced so severe an attack of
gout, that from December till Easter he suffered
from it extremely, although the régime and diet he
submitted to for the first time were most severe:
this was his eleventh attack of gout.

The Emperor had intended visiting Germany
about this time to restore order.* For it must be
known that, since the year 1529, when, as already
stated, he visited Italy for the first time, and had an
interview with Pope Clement, he never ceased whenever he saw either Pope Clement or Pope Paul, and
in every journey, and at every Diet in Germany, and

* Para trattar de seu remedio.

at every time and opportunity, continually to solicit, either personally or through his ministers, the con- vocation of a general council to provide a remedy for the evils which had arisen in Germany, and for the errors which were being propagated in Chris- tendom.*

As regards Pope Clement, owing to various diffi- culties of a personal nature, and despite the promise he had made to His Majesty to convoke such a council within the delay of one year, it was never possible to make him fulfil it.† His successor Pope Paul declared at the commencement of his Pontificate that he had promised to announce and convoke the council immediately, and exhibited a lively desire to provide a remedy for the evils which had befallen Christianity, and for the abuses of the Church; nevertheless those demonstrations and first zeal gradually cooled down, and, following the steps and the example of Pope Clement, he temporised

---

* Porque heder saber, que como ja se disse, desde anno 29 que foi a primeira vez que passou a Italia e se via com o Papa Clemente nunqua deixou todas as vezes, que se vio assi com o mesmo Papa Clemente como com o Papa Paulo, e em todas seus caminhos, e dietas, que tinha feito na ditta Germania, e em todos os outros tempos e occasioes de continuamente sollicitar hora em persoa, hora per meio de seus ministros, concilio geral para remedio da ditta Germania e dos erros, que iam multiplicando na Christandade.

† Quanto ao Papa Clemente, por algús inconvenientes, che havia em sua pessoa, sem embargo da promessa, que tinha feito a Sua Magestade de dentro de hum anno convocar o ditto concilio, ja mais foi possivel accabar com elle, que o quisesse executar.

with soft words, and always postponed the convocation and meeting of the council,* until, as already
observed above, he sent to Monzon, where the King
of France commenced the war in 1542—a bull of
convocation of the said council at Trent. The time
and opportunity show what his real intentions were.
God knows them, and they are easily discernible in
what then took place, and by His Majesty's reply.†
Nevertheless, in consequence of changes which occurred in affairs—changes far different from what
had been calculated upon by discerning minds—
matters were arranged,‡ and were in such guise
conducted that the said convocation was held. The
council met and continued for a long time to sit at
Trent, until the said Pope Paul, from certain reasons
(God will it that they were good ones!) wished to
transfer it to Bologna.§ His Holiness therefore,

---

* A Papa Paulo, ainda que no princípio de seu Pontificado pub-
licasse que tinha promettido de logo publicar e convocar concilio, e
mostrasse grandes desejos de remediar a Christendada e abusos da
Igrega, com tudo despois com o tempo aquellas mostras e ardor primeiro se foi es friando, e seguiado os passos e exemplo do Papa
Clemente, com boas palavras prolongou, e entretene sempre a con-
voçáõ e ajuntamente do concilio.

† A sazáõ e opportunidade do tempo mostram bem, com que
tençáõ isto era, e Deus o sabe, e pelo que entáõ passou, e sua
Magestade respondeo, se pode claramente entender.

‡ Con tudo polas mudanças que nos negocios sobrevieram bem
differentas do que algús agudos engenhos tinháo discorrido, as cousas
se ordenaram.

§ Atee que o ditto Papa Paulo por r⸱　　　　ι (os

entertaining towards the Emperor the sentiments
alluded to above, and seizing the opportunity of the
propositions made by His Majesty at the Diet of
Spires, addressed to him a brief, little in accordance
with the sentiments which His Majesty had professed
during the whole of his life.* The Emperor declined
giving a reply, as it could not be done without com-
promising the honour and authority of the two heads
of Christianity, and he was much grieved that the
Protestants took advantage of this opportunity to
reply to the Pope in the name of His Majesty.† The
Emperor followed up what had been resolved upon
at the Diet of Spires relative to the assembling of
another Diet at Worms; but this latter having been
convoked, the Emperor, in consequence of being laid
up, could not proceed there on the day appointed.
He therefore requested the King his brother to go
there in his stead; and he also sent M. de Granvelle
there that they might attend it and hasten to discuss

quaes Deus que forsem bons) trattou do avocar e transferir a
Bolonha.

* E tendo Sua Santitade 'para com o Emperador a tencáõ, que
acima se mostrou, e tomando occasiáõ da prattica, que Sua Magestade
fes na dieta de Spira, che escreveo hum breve bem differente de
profissam, que Sua Magestade fizera toda sua vida.

† Ao qual Sua Magestade não quis responder por quanto se não
podia bem fazer, guardando o decora e aucthoridade das duas
cabeças da Christandade, e lhe pezou bem da occasiáõ, que com
grande audacia tomaram as protestantes de lhe responder em nome
de Sua Magestade.

and settle the business in hand, adopting the best expedient possible.*

1545   With the object above mentioned in view, the Emperor left Brussels for Antwerp, although still suffering from the gout and the medical treatment he had undergone, and there he received a visit from M. d'Orleans. Leaving, for the fourth time, the Queen of Hungary, his sister, Governor of the states of Flanders, he proceeded by the Rhine to Worms. This was the seventh time that the Emperor performed this journey. He entered Germany with the intention and lively desire to remedy what was taking place, which he hoped to do more easily by means of some amicable arrangement, as he was at peace with the King of France, and there was no appearance of the Turk attacking Germany. But as he knew and had seen the great arrogance and the obstinacy of the Protestants, he feared that no good result would be obtained.† He had always maintained the conviction, with many others, that it was impossible to lower by means of severity such obstinacy and so great a power as that possessed by the Protestants: he was therefore perplexed how to act in a matter which it was so necessary and so important to see settled.‡

* E indo ganhando tempo encaminharem e ordinarem as cousas tomando o mais breve e melhor expediente que podesse ser.

† Mas como Sua Magestade tinha entendido e visto a grande soberba e obstinaçaõ dos protestantes, receava que por virtude nenhũa cousa fizessem, que conveniente fosse.

‡ E por quanto Sua Magestade tivera sempre, e muitos outros

But God, who never forsakes those who have recourse
unto Him, even when they do not deserve it,* was not
satisfied with granting the grace to the Emperor to
give him Gueldres so promptly. The experience of
what was occurring also opened the Emperor's eyes
and enlightened his mind, so that no longer did it
seem to him impossible to subjugate such pride by
force, but on the contrary it seemed to him most
easy, under suitable circumstances and by proper
means.† As this matter was one of the highest importance and of such great weight, he would not
take upon himself to decide it, and he communicated
it only (because of the secrecy it was necessary to
maintain) to a few of his most trustworthy ministers,
who had experience of the past, and to whom in
consequence he communicated his plans.‡ Their
advice agreed with His Majesty's opinion, but the

---

tinham para si que via impossivel per via de força abaixar hum táŏ
obstinado e grande poder, qual era a que os protestantes tinham, se
achava perplexo acerca do que poderia fazer, por remediar cousa que
tanta convinha importava.

* Mas Deus que jamais desampara aquelles, que a elle recorrem,
ainda que o não mereçam.

† Mas como a experiencia do que possava lhe abrio os olhos, e
allumiou o entendimento de sorte, que dalli pordiante não soo não
lhe pareceo impossivel, poder per via de força domar tao grande soberba, mas o teve por muy facil, emprendendo o em tempo e modo
conveniente.

‡ E por o negocio ser de grande importancia e peso, não querendo
fiar de si, soo a resolução delle, a communicou com algús poucos de
seus ministros mais fleis por cousa do segredo, que convinha se
tivesse, e que tambem tinham experiencia do passado, aos quaes por
cousa della se representou o mesmo.

Emperor postponed the execution of the plan, hoping that it would be sanctioned by the Diet of Worms, and foreseeing that in default of restoring order in Germany by quiet and pacific means it would be necessary to have recourse to arms, according to circumstances and opportunities.*

The Emperor, as already said, continued his journey to Worms, where he found but few princes of the empire, but many representatives or commissaries with whom he commenced negotiating, continuing what had already been concluded in a conference previously held in the same city. But the slackness and carelessness which they displayed in this negotiation clearly denoted with what intentions and in what spirit they treated these matters.† The Emperor, perceiving this, communicated his idea and the considerations explained above to the King of the Romans, his brother, who had come to the Diet as a brother and a prince much interested in this question.‡ The latter, with the zeal which he displayed in all things connected

* E Sua Magestade deixou a execução para quando e conforme ao que se podesse resolver na dieta de Vormes, porque não podendo por bons meios e modos pacificamente reduzir Alemanha, então se viria as armas e força, segundo e tempo e opportunidade que se offerecesse.

† D'onde se seguia tão fraca e fria negociação, que se via claramente, com que tenção e animo se trattava de taes negocios.

‡ O que vendo Sua Magestade e vindo nesto tempo á dieta el Rey de Romanos, seu irmão como a irmão e a quem o negocio grandemente toccava, communicou seu parecer a discurso acima ditto.

with the service of God, and with a great desire to
remedy such great evils, seeing the obstinacy of the
Protestants, and the small or no results that were
obtained by acting towards them by measures of
kindness, approved the Emperor's project as practicable, and agreed to it.* The Emperor considered
that time and opportunity were propitious and
favourable to the accomplishment of this project,
and that to this end it was proper and necessary that
he should have the support of the spiritual and
temporal power of the Pope, as being the person
most concerned in putting in order and procuring a
remedy for such great evils.† Their Majesties therefore agreed upon it between them, swearing to
secrecy, and on the condition that, should the secret
not be kept, they should not be bound to what might
have been revealed; and they resolved to communi-
cate their determination to Cardinal Farnèse, grandson and legate of Pope Paul, who, at this period,

---

* O qual com o fervor que tem nas cousas, que são de serviço de
Deus, e grande desejo do remedio de tão grandes males, vendo a
obstinação dos protestantes, e o pouco ou nenhum effecto, que se
seguia de proceder com elles per modos e termos brandos, achou o
ditto discurso do Emperador, fundado em razão e possibilidade, e se
conformou com elle.

† E considerando, que o tempo e opportanidade era mui propicia
e accommodada para executar o ditto discurso, e que para este effeito
convinha a era necessario que o Papa concorresse e ajudasse com suas
forças spirituaes e temporaes, como aquelle que estava mais obrigado
a dar ordem e procurar remedio a tantos males.

arrived in the city of Worms.* Consequently, after
having sworn to secrecy, and accepted the above-
mentioned condition, they communicated to him
that, if His Holiness would, as has been said, give
them the support of his spiritual and temporal
power, their Majesties, considering that kind and
conciliating measures were of no avail, and that the
obstinacy and the insolence of the Protestants increased daily to such a degree that it could no longer
be tolerated, would undertake by force to remedy
and obviate their obstinacy and their insolence.†
Cardinal Farnèse was so startled at this overture
that, although he had previously declared that he
was provided with full powers to discuss everything
connected with the remedy for existing evils, he
would not take any steps in going further into the
conclusion of this matter.‡ And as their Majesties

* Suas Magestades assentaram ambos entre si, de com juramento de
segredo e condiçáõ, que se este se não guardasse, elles não estariam
obrigados a cousa, che tivessem ditta, e offerecida communicar sua
determinaçáõ com o cardeal Farnes, neto e entonces legado do Papa
Paulo, que neste tempo chegou ao mesmo lugar de Vormes.

† E assi, despois que declaron a Suas Magestades com o juramento
e condiçáõ dantes ditta lhe proposeram e offerecevão que se Sua
Santidade quisesse ajudar, como ditto he, com suas forçãs spirituaes
e temporaes (visto com os modos e meios suaves e de concordia não
tínham lugar, e a obstinaçáõ e insolencia dos protestantes ia cada dia
crescendo de sorte que se não podia ja soffrer) Suas Magestades em-
prenderiam por via di força remediar e obviar a taes obstinaçoés e
insolencia

‡ Do qual offerecimento o ditto Cardeal ficou táõ espantado, que
dizendo dantes, que trazia amplos poderes para trattar de tudo o que

said that, as he would not take any farther steps nor
take any resolution upon himself, it would be best to
consult His Holiness without delay by an express
messenger who would bring back his reply, he posi-
tively declined to do anything, but he wished himself
to be the messenger, saying that he would make
good haste; and in fact it was such as suited a person
of his authority, but not such as the importance of the
matter demanded.* The first thing he did on arriving
at Rome was to go against his oath, and against the
condition imposed by His Majesty. In fact, His
Holiness immediately convoked a consistory, where
there are always conflicting opinions and parties, and
he communicated to it the offers of the Emperor.†
The Pope chose as his legate the same Cardinal
Farnèse, and as Gonfaloniere or General of the
Church his brother Duke Octavio; other captains
and officers were immediately appointed; the drum

tocasse ao remedio dos presentes males, não quis passar mais ao
diante na conclusão deste negocio.

* E dizendo lhe Suas Magestades, que ja que não possava mais
avante, não querendo per si concluir nada, o melhor seria consultar
com toda diligencia Sua Santidade per hum proprio, que lhe
trouxesse a resposta, de nenhum modo o quis fazer, mas elle mesmo
quis ser o messageiro, dizendo que faria boa diligencia, a qual foi tal
qual a hum personagem de sua auchtoridade convinha, mas não a que
a qualidade de negocio requeria.

† Porque tanto que chegou a Roma, a primeira cousa que se fez
foi ir em tudo contra o juramento e condição, que Sua Magestade
tinha posto; porque logo Sua Santidade chamou o consistorio onde
sempre costuma haver opinoés e bandos contrarios, as qual communicou o offerecimento.

* G

was beaten to bring men to the Papal standard, calling upon them to join this holy expedition and avenge the sack of Rome.*

His Majesty considering that, when the above proposal was made to Cardinal Farnèse, it was near the festival of St. John, and that with all the speed the Cardinal could display the reply would arrive too late and the season would be too far advanced to commence assembling an army, and to make the necessary preparations for so great an undertaking, presuming also that the secret would not be kept, sent an express to His Holiness representing to him that the plan could not be carried out this year, but that it was necessary the secret should be kept close, as otherwise he should not hold himself bound by the offers he had made.† As the secret was violated, and as the Protestants were warned, the Emperor thought fit to act in such a manner that they added no faith to the report which was circulated.‡   The

---

* Publicando que vinham a esta sancta empresa e a tomar vingança do Sacco de Roma.

† Vendo Sua Magestade Imperial que quando proposo acima ditto ao Cardial Farnes era pelo St. Jao, e que conforme a dilegencia que o ditto Cardeal podia fazer, a resposta veria ja fora de tempo e em sazáö muito adeantado para começar a trattar de por em ordem o exercito, e apprector as cousas convenientes a tal negocio, presumindo tambem que o segredo se não guardaria, despachou hum proprio a Sua Santidade advertido o que por este anno a ditta determinaçáö se não podia executar e que por tanto se guardasse bem o segredo, porque d'outra maneira não se tinha por obrigado aos offerecimentos que fizera.

‡ E por quanto o segredo se rompeo, e os protestantes foram

Emperor also saw that at the said Diet nothing would be done except to waste time (he however wished it to sit until he had received the Pope's answer), and he confined himself to short and curt communications,* postponing the negotiations for a Diet convoked to meet the following year at Ratisbon.

Meantime a conference was held in the same city as to the best means for remedying these differences.† During this Diet the Emperor received the news that the Princess of Spain, his daughter-in-law, had been delivered of a son, who was afterwards called Don Carlos, and four or five days afterwards he received the very different news of the death of the same Princess, which naturally caused him great grief. At the same time the King of the Romans also received the news of the death of his eldest daughter, which afflicted the Emperor as much as if he had been her own father.

All these things terminated, the Emperor left Worms, and for the eighth time, taking the Rhine route, he returned for the seventh time to the Netherlands, where he found the Queen of Hungary his sister at Louvain, and from thence he proceeded to Brussels, where he received the news of the death of

advertidos, se teve contudo tal modo, que a fama que corria não foi per elles corda.

* Lhe fez hira breve e serra prattica.

† No mesma lugar se fez hum colloquio a cerca dos modos, que poderia haver para remedio destas differenças.

the Duke of Orleans, eight days before the anni-
versary of the peace of Crespy, one of the conditions
of which was, that the duchy was to be conferred
upon him. This death came opportunely, for, as
it was natural, it may be believed that God had
resolved it in His secret judgements.*

* A qual morte veo a tempo, que sendo natural pode parecer, que
foi ordenada de Deus por seus secretos juizos.

CHAPTER VI.

The Emperor proceeds to Bruges. — Charles holds a Chapter of the
Golden Fleece at Utrecht. — Visits the Duchy of Gueldres. — The
Electors request Explanations respecting a League against the Pro-
testants.—The Emperor denies its Existence. — Progress of the Re-
formation.—The Smalcalde League.—The Diet of Ratisbon.—The
Pope's Emissaries endeavour to persuade the Emperor to take up
Arms. — Duke William of Bavaria joins the Secret League. —
The Protestants prepare for the worst. — Charles concludes an
Armistice with the Turk. — Commencement of Hostilities against
the Protestants. — The Protestants capture Füssen and Clusa. —
Charles resolves, living or dead, to remain Emperor of Germany.
—The Emperor marches on Neustadt.

THE Emperor now proceeded to Bruges, where
different grand personages arrived both from
France as well as from England, charged, in consequence of this change, to modify, correct, and draw
up anew the conventions concluded between the
three monarchs;* but, not being able to come to
any agreement on the subject, they had recourse to
the expedients that suited them best. And henceforth the treaties of peace concluded between their
Majesties were maintained as much by the dissimu-
lation of some as by the tolerance of others.†

* Para per occasiáõ desta mudança, innovar, mudar, e fazer de
novo.
† Assi pola dissimulaçaõ d'algúas d'ellas, come pola tolerancia
d'outras.

This done, the Emperor left for Bois-le-Duc, to
proceed from thence to Utrecht to hold a Chapter
of the Golden Fleece. But at Bois-le-Duc he was
attacked by the gout, so that he was obliged to
remain there, and to postpone the Chapter to some
other time. Shortly afterwards, feeling better, he
held it at Utrecht, where he had a relapse. The
Chapter over, and having somewhat recovered, he
left Utrecht to visit his possessions in the state of
Gueldres, which he occupied again in virtue of his
ancient claim to it. The necessity he was under of
taking the field against his enemies had prevented
him from going there at the time the duchy was restored to him. Having paid this visit, he continued
his journey as far as Maestricht, still very weak from
his last attack of gout, which was the twelfth. In
this city he received deputies from some of the
Electors and Princes of the empire. They said that
they had been informed that His Majesty was coming to Germany at the head of an army — something
quite new, and which scandalised the greater portion
of that country.* They explained their mission on the
grounds of a report in circulation, and which had its
origin in what had taken place at Rome in the preceding year at the time of the journey of Cardinal

* Dizendo, que foram advertidos, que Sua Magestade vinha com
mão armada a Germania, cousa nova, e que muito escalandissava a
maior parte della.

left, he would endeavour to bring them back to
Ratisbon, where a Diet had been convoked, he
nevertheless did nothing of the sort, and the conference was broken up and dissolved. The Emperor
therefore continued his journey to Ratisbon. There
he found only the commissioners of the states of the
empire, but not a single prince; but the Elector of
Mayence arrived there a few days afterwards, as
much on private business as respecting the convocation of the Diet, as a short time previously he had
been elected, on the death of the Cardinal, Elector of
Mayence. However this may be, the Emperor was
obliged to open the Diet, and to make his proposals
to those who were present; but they were received
so coldly, matters were treated with so much negligence, and the Protestants continued to display so
much arrogance, that the Emperor came to the
decided conviction that measures of kindness would
be of little avail, and that he would be compelled,
much against his inclination, to have recourse to
more rigorous measures.*

At this time the Pope's emissaries and some
ecclesiastics were incessantly endeavouring to induce the Emperor to take up arms against the

* A qual foi tão friamente tomada e os negocios com tão grande
negligencia trattados, e pelos protestantes continuada hũa tão grande
arrogancia, que Sua Magestade julgava e via claramente, que os re-
medios brandos serviram de pouco, e ainda que muito contra sua
vontade, seria forçado usar d'outros mais fortes.

Protestants.* His Majesty, however, hesitated, as
much on account of the greatness and difficulty of
such an enterprise, as also to have time to consult
the King his brother, whom he daily expected.† As
already stated, the secret had been badly kept; the
Protestants were on their guard, and were commencing
their preparations and armaments, not wishing to be
taken by surprise; they even thought of surprising the
others.‡ The Emperor was unwilling to do anything
to create agitation in Germany, but all admitted that
any further delay on his part might make him lose
many advantages which he might otherwise obtain.§
As soon as his brother the King had arrived, he
made him acquainted with the exact state of affairs;
and as a long time previously Duke William of
Bavaria had offered his services, requesting and
endeavouring to persuade their Majesties to take up
arms, as the sole remedy for so much insolence,‖

---

* Neste tempo os ministros do Papa e algús ecclesiasticos não
cessaram de sollicitar ao Emperador, que quisesse concluir os concertos com seu amo, e começar de tomar as armas contra os protestantes.

† O que todavia Sua Magestade dilatava assi pola grandeza e
difficuldade da empresa, como por se resolver com el Rey seu irmão.

‡ Porque, como ditto he, o segredo se guardara mal, e os protestantes andavam sobre aviso, e começavam de se prover e armar,
como aquelles, que não soomente não quersam ser tomados desaper-
cebidos, mas ainda trattavam de tomar aos outros descuidados.

§ O que Sua Magestade não tinha feito per menos alterar a Ger-
manía atee que todas viram que não podia o fazer, e que por ter tanto
esperado, perdera muito da ventagem, que podera ter.

‖ Como muito tempo antes o Duque Guilhelmo de Bavera se tinha

their Majesties entered into negotiations with him
to induce him to join the alliance or league proposed
by the emissaries of the Pope; * but, notwithstanding
the zeal and energy he at first had displayed in this
matter, he cooled down so much, that he was the
cause that its conclusion was postponed longer than
was necessary.† At last an alliance was made with
him, from which little profit was derived except that
his country supplied the Imperial army with provisions. The churchmen were also called upon to
come forward and join the League. But when it
came to the point of assembling and adopting a
conclusion, though they had displayed immense zeal
before, their hearts failed them, either from fear of the
Protestants, or from reluctance to enter into so great
an enterprise, or from other considerations, and they
did not venture to join the League.‡ They consented,
however, to contribute a sum of money, in virtue of
an agreement passed in preceding Diets, a contribu-
tion to which the Protestants not only did not hold

offerecido, incitando e induzido Suas Magestades a tomar as arma s
como unico remedio de tantas insolencias.

  * No concerto, ou ligua, que os do Papa sollicitaram e offereciam.

  † Mas mostrando se de principio táõ sollicito e quente no negocio,
se esfrion de sorte, que por sua causa se dilatou a conciusáõ mais
doque convinha.

  ‡ Os quaes da mesma maneira antes de vir a obra, se tinham
mostrado muito desejos, mas quando se veo ajúntar e concluir, ou
por receo que tivessem dos protestantes, ou per medo d'entrar em
húa táõ grande cousa, ou por outros respeitos, não se aventuraram,
nem atreveram e entrar na liga.

themselves bound, but which moreover they opposed,* preventing many from paying their share.
Thus the Protestants, by these preparations, had
gained the advantage which the Emperor might have
had over them had the secret been well kept. From
all these reasons this affair incurred great difficulties
and risks. Yet the Emperor felt that it would be
difficult to avoid carrying out what had been agreed
upon, that time was being lost, and that the longer
it was delayed the more public would it become,
the more difficult and perilous.† He, moreover, took
into consideration, as already said, that he was at
peace with France, and that King Francis was much
hampered by the war he was waging with the King
of England;‡ that it was rumoured that the Turk
was engaged in wars at home; that consequently it
might be presumed, with some probability, that no
danger was to be feared from that quarter. Moreover, to make matters more sure, the Emperor and the

* Do qual os protestantes não soo não fizeram caso para contri-
buirem, mas antes contra vinham, e ião a mão a algûs por pagarem
sua parte.

† Assi ainda que polo apparalho dantes ditto, os protestantes tinham
ganhado e tomado a ventagem sobre o Emperador, que elle podera
tomar sobre elles, se segredo se não rompera, e por todas estas cousas
o negocio ficava mais difficultoso e arriscado, com tudo vendo Sua
Magestade, que ja mal se podia escusar d'execução do que estava trattado, e que o tempo se hia passando e que quanto mais se tardava,
tanto a cousa mais se publicava,difficultava e se fazia mais perigosa.

‡ E el Rey Francisco may gastado por causa da guerra que teve com
el Rey d'Inglaterra.

King of the Romans had sent emissaries to the Turk
to negotiate, should such a step seem advisable, an
armistice with him, which in fact was afterwards
concluded. He moreover observed that the Protestants had cast off all shame, and were actively
enlisting troops, with a view to accomplish their
designs.* Their Majesties therefore resolved to
conclude with the Pope, and put into execution that
which necessity compelled them to do, and which
had been the object of such lengthened negotiations.†
In fact, matters had already so far advanced, that had
the Emperor not gone into the enterprise, the organ-
isation of the Protestants would have enabled them
to carry out the plan recommended by the Landgrave,
as narrated before.‡

Immediately after the arrival of the King at
Ratisbon, the Queen, his wife, came there with her
daughters; and Duke William of Bavaria and Duke
William of Clèves also arrived with their wives and
children, and other princes of the empire. In the

---

* E considerando ultimamente que os protestantes tindam ja de
todo perdido o vergonha e com toda a pressa faziam gente, e punham
por obro seus desenhos.

† Se determinaram Suas Magestades de concluir com o Papa, e dar
execuçaõ a que a necessidade os obrigava, e estava trattado havia
tanto tempo.

‡ Por que as cousas estavam ja tanto avante, que se o Emperador
não dèra principio a empresa, os protestantes estavam em tal ordem,
que poderam por em execuçaõ o conselho, que dantes se disse, que o
Lantsgrave lhes tinha dado.

same city were celebrated the nuptials of Duke Albert of Bavaria and of Duke William of Clèves with two daughters of the King and Queen of the Romans. When the nuptials were over, the Queen and her daughters, the dukes and duchesses, and newly-married couples, left. Then the King and Duke Maurice took their departure to attack, each on their side, the lands of John Frederick of Saxony, which they carried out in such guise that, after defeating his army, they took from him a large portion of his domains. It was at Ratisbon that the Emperor commenced assembling his army, entering into negotiations for that purpose with various princes, captains, and warriors; so that in a few days he assembled a certain number of German soldiers, who were joined by the Spaniards who were in Hungary.

The principal towns of Suabia, which belonged to the League of Smalcalde, had previously received a letter written by the Emperor, in which he told them that he was informed that they were assembling troops, in consequence of a report which was spread that he intended to wage war against them for the sake of religion, and in which he assured them that the report was false, that he had not entertained the idea of waging war, especially against those who had obeyed him, and who had done nothing against the Imperial authority, and that consequently, if they disbanded their army and gave proof of obedience, they might come to terms with His Majesty; but the deputies which they sent about this time showed so much obstinacy, and in their insolence they replied with so much arrogance, that His Majesty dismissed them as they deserved.* In like mannei the Protestant commissioners who were at the Diet waited one day upon His Majesty, and, referring to the rumours of war that were in circulation, requested him to make known his intentions.† His Majesty replied to them that he did not wish to go to war, unless compelled to do so to uphold his authority, which was daily attacked and attempted to be lowered and diminished.‡ As soon as they had received this reply, all the Protestants withdrew

---

* Neste tempo os deputados das principaes cidades de Suevia, que eram da liga Esmalcaldiana, sobre hûa carta, que o Emperador escrevera dizendo lhes, como fora avisado, que faziam gente de guerra por algua fama que corria, que lhes queria fazer guerra por causa da religiáõ, assegurando lhe qua tal fama era falsa, e que elle não tinha pensamento de fazer tal cousa, principalmente contra aquelles, que lhe fossem obedientes, e não fizessem contra a aucthoridade Imperial, e que por tanto s' elles eram destes, desfizessem o exercito, e se mostrassem obedientes, vieram ter com Sua Magestade, es com grande obstinaçáõ em sua insolencia responderam mui soberbamente. O que vendo o Emperador, os despedio, como elles mereciam.

† E propondo lhe a fama, que corria de guerra, pediram que os certificasse de sua tençáõ.

‡ Que elle não queria fazer guerra senáõ forçado por conservar sua aucthoridade, contra a qual via que cada dia se attentava, e trabalhava pola abaixar e deminuir.

without even taking leave.[*] The Emperor, seeing
that the Diet might already be considered as terminated and broken up, had a short and curt
explanation with those who remained.[†] Then the
men of arms that the said towns had levied were
taken to Füssen, under the pretext of preventing the
entrance of foreign soldiers into Germany. They
took Füssen and another fortress called Clusa, which
belonged to the King of the Romans, so that they
were the first to commence hostilities and open the
war.[‡] They also committed a serious error in their
bad designs and evil inspirations, by taking that
road instead of that of Ratisbon (it was the second
error that they committed by the will of God who
blinded them); for at this period His Majesty was
not yet in a position to offer them any formidable resistance.[§] The Emperor, aware that the
Italians, whom the Pope had sent under the orders
of Cardinal Farnèse, as his Legate, and of Duke
Octavio as his Gonfaloniere, were on their way, as

---

[*] E tendo esta resposta todos os protestantes se foram sem dizerem:
A Deus.

[†] Com os que ficaram fez hûa breve o serra prattica.

[‡] De modo que elles foram os primeiros, que começaram a offender
e a romper a guerra.

[§] E não erraram pouco por seguir sua maa tenção, e maos prin-
cipios em tomar antes este caminho, que o de Ratisbona (e foi este
o segundo erro que fizeram por permissão de Deus, que os cegou) por
que Sua Magestade não estava ainda aquelle tempo bem apercebido
para lhes resistir, como convinha.

also the Spaniards, who were to come to Lombardy,
considered what difficulties they would have to en-
counter in forming a junction with him; he also
observed that John Frederick of Saxony and the
Landgrave were already at Donauwerth with their
whole army, and that if they were to place themselves between His Majesty and his troops, those
forces would be divided, and each corps consequently
weaker; and although some of his advisers were
scrupulous, out of respect for His Majesty's reputa-
tion, about leaving Ratisbon, the Emperor paid no
heed to such vanities.* He was decided when he conceived this enterprise with the principal object which
determined him to do so, to lead it to a successful
issue whatever might happen, as he resolved, living
or dead, to remain Emperor in Germany.† He
therefore resolved to quit Ratisbon, leaving it provided with a good garrison, and to proceed to Land-
shut, a town of the Duke of Bavaria. He arrived
there with the few troops that were with him; but,
seeing the multitude of enemies that awaited him
there, he held council with the Duke of Alba, whom
he had appointed his Captain-General, and with other

* Não fazendo caso destas vaidades.

† Estando determinado quando propos de seguir esta emprese,
vista a causa principal por que a emprendia, de vir ao fim della,
qualquer cousa que ouvesse d'accontecer, por que tinha proposto e
assentado dentro de si, vivo ou morto, ficar Emperador em Alemanha.

captains, as to the best fortified position to occupy, and the best measures to be adopted, as well to resist the enemy, as to await the arrival of his troops, who, in consequence of the length and difficulty of the journey, did not arrive so promptly as all desired.

At this time the Protestants who had taken Rhain, a domain of the Duke of Bavaria, were advancing on Ingolstadt, a town belonging to the same duke, into which the Emperor had placed some troops. They sent him by a trumpeter and a page, according to their custom, a letter, as long as it was insolent, of which His Majesty took no heed, and to which he did not take the trouble to reply.* As they had entered into this path, it would have been better for them if they had adhered to their defiance, throwing off all reserve and carrying out their threats, than to waste their time in such empty fanfaronades.† God blinded them; he allowed this to be the third fault which they committed, that they might not obtain the object of their perverse designs.‡ The Emperor,

---

* Lhe mandaram per hum trombeta e hum page, conforme seu costume, húa carta bem comprida, e não menos desavergonhada, da qual Sua Magestade nem tomou pena de lhe responde.

† Melhor fora para elles, ja que estavam postos em tal caminho, de seguir sua pouca vergonha no cartel, e executar os fios, de que nelle usavam, que despois de se terem mostrado tão bravos e insoentes firarem quaes ficarem.

‡ Deus os cegou e permittio, que esta fosse a terceira falta, que lelles commetteram por não chegar ao fim de sua perversa tenção.

turning this time and advantage to account,* hastened
the arrival of the Papal troops, as well as of those of
the other Italian princes, of the Spaniards, who had
been called from Lombardy, and of some Germans,
who, in consequence of impediments and obstacles
caused by the advance of the Protestants, had not
been able to arrive sooner. They all reached Land-
shut, and the Emperor immediately commenced to
march with all the troops he had assembled, in the
direction of Neustadt, a town belonging to the Duke
of Bavaria, with the intention and wish of establish-
ing his head-quarters there, to entrench himself and
gradually approach the enemy, which he could not
do at the present moment, from a scarcity of provisions, because, as the war had only just commenced,
the necessary measures had not yet been completed
to provide the army abundantly with all that it
stood in need of. Consequently the Emperor left
Neustadt for Ratisbon; and there he so well organised matters, that no further want of provisions
was felt; at least nothing worth mentioning. In the
same city arrived the Spaniards, who came from
Naples by the Adriatic; and also Marquises John
and Albert of Brandenburg, and the Master of
Prussia, with all the German cavalry they could
collect, thereby rendering service to His Majesty.†

* E assi tendo dado esta commodidada e espaço ao Emperador.
† D'onde Sua Magestade tinha bem que fazer.

CHAPTER VII.

The War with the Protestants. — Charles crosses the Danube. —
The Protestants at Ingolstadt. — Count de Buren. — Position of the
Emperor's Army. — A Night Assault. — The Protestants bombard
the Imperial Camp for eight consecutive Hours. — Retreat of the
Protestants. — Surrender of Neuburg. — The Emperor arrives at
Maresheim. — Hears Mass in the Expectation of a great Battle. —
The Protestants occupy the Heights near Nördlingen. — The
Emperor prepares for Battle. — Is dissuaded from crossing the
River. — The Duke of Brunswick is killed in a Skirmish. — Sur-
render of Donauwerth to the Emperor.

NEVERTHELESS the Protestants imagined in
their arrogance that the Emperor was beating a
retreat, and getting away from them, and they crossed
to the other side of the Danube to occupy the hills,
which, on that side, dominate Ratisbon, so as to bring
their artillery into play, which they held in high account,* against the Emperor's army, which had its
quarters there, and could not take up any others,
except on the banks of the river. But the Emperor,
having, as already said, made all his arrangements for
provisions, and not wishing to lose time or remain
distant from his foes,† left Ratisbon, and proceeded

---

* Para dalli jogar da artilharjia, de que elles faziam grande caso.
† E não querendo perder tempo, nem es tar longe de seus adver-
sarios.

by marches to Neustadt. Whilst he was on the road, his enemies took the one which we have indicated higher up, and they arrived within three leagues of Ratisbon; but finding that their plan had failed, and that they were marching through a difficult and mountainous country, they feared lest the Emperor should attack them in the flank, and cut off their supplies. They therefore retraced their steps as quickly as they could, to gain a narrow and difficult pass near a place called Perengries, at two German leagues' distance from Neustadt, at which latter place, as already stated, the Emperor had arrived with his army. In consequence of not having been informed of the enemy's movements by those who were aware of them, and whose duty it was to give the information * of the advantage he would have had in attacking the enemy in a spot so disadvantageous for them, the Emperor lost an excellent opportunity; but it was not through his fault.†

His Majesty now crossed the Danube, and pitched his camp in an excellent and strong position opposite Neustadt. The enemy, having got through the defile already mentioned, continued their march, and encamped near the Danube, at two leagues nearer to Neuburg than to Ingolstadt. The Emperor

---

* Por falta de não ser advirtido per aquelles que sabdam, podiam e o deviam advirtir.

† Que todavia se não perdeo por sua culpa.

was anxious to attack them, despite the great dis-
proportion of strength,* as much with a view daily
to gain ground, as to facilitate the movements of
M. de Buren, whom he had charged to assemble a large
number of Germans, both horse and foot, which he
had done, bringing with him also other German
horsemen, sent by Duke Henry of Brunswick and
other captains in the service of the Emperor. This
cavalry, which the Protestants had prevented passing,
had, from this reason, joined M. de Buren, to advance with him and join His Majesty together. The
Emperor, carrying out his intention and above-
mentioned plan, left the camp near Neustadt, to
assume a position near Ingolstadt, where he would
have his face turned towards the enemy,† the Danube
on his left, the town of Ingolstadt in his rear, and
on his right an open plain. But as this position
offered some difficulties, the Emperor had another
excellent and strong one in reserve between Neustadt
and Ingolstadt. The Emperor having made a reconnaissance of the one he had the intention of occupying before Ingolstadt, sent some light horse to
skirmish as far as the enemy's camp, which had the
effect of making them move; and it was deemed
certain that they were advancing straight to take
up a position close to the encampment which His

---

* Ainda que se arhava bem differente em forças.
† A cara para o campo dos enemigos.

Majesty had resolved to occupy: this they could easily have done, because they were much nearer to the spot, and were greatly superior in numbers. This induced the Emperor to halt and establish his camp in the locality which he had kept in reserve, as already said, until he had exactly ascertained the enemy's intentions. Finding that they returned to the quarters which they had left, he immediately advanced with his army, and occupied the position he wished to take before Ingolstadt; and he did so with such speed, that he arrived there, though at a late hour, the same day. During the whole of this night (which did not pass without some noise, as the multitude who followed could scarcely find their quarters in the dark) he ordered trenches to be dug, in so far as time allowed it; and what could not be done during the night was completed, as far as possible, at daybreak.

For some days the two camps remained close to and opposite each other, and a few skirmishes took place, in which, with God's blessing, the enemy always had the worst of it.* Nevertheless, they came and established themselves one league nearer to His Majesty. A night assault caused them great damage, and on the following day a good skirmish ensued; on the day following that, very early in the morning,

---

* Sempre levaram o peor.

they advanced with the whole of their army and artillery in good order, within cannon-range, towards the Imperial camp. The Emperor, having been immediately informed of this by his general, the Duke of Alba, donned his armour, mounted his charger, and ordered the duke at once, without making any noise or causing any alarm,* to put the whole army in order of battle. The Emperor had scarcely shown himself, and the order which he had given had scarcely been executed, when the enemy, who had already established a portion of their artillery on a ridge, which was very convenient for them for this purpose, opened fire with that artillery, and with a number of other guns placed at different points, upon the camp and army of the Emperor, with such good will, that from eight o'clock in the morning till four o'clock in the afternoon, they fired from eight hundred to nine hundred rounds of heavy artillery; an event hitherto unprecedented, for never had an army in the open field been exposed to such a fire, without being protected by entrenchments. Nevertheless, the soldiers of the Emperor supported it so well that not one of them displayed the slightest semblance of fear, and, by God's blessing, the said artillery did not do much harm. The enemy suffered much more from the artillery with which the Imperial

---

* Sem estrôndo e sem torcar alarma.

army replied to them. It was reported that they
had the plan of ceasing the fire of their artillery and
attacking the Emperor's camp. It is possible that
they had good reason not to do so; at all events,
they must not be blamed for not having done so.*

Thus passed this day, and the enemy returned to
their quarters which, meantime, they had repaired.

The Emperor ordered all his men to sleep in the
trenches, that, on any alarm, the horsemen should
proceed on foot to the trenches, and that everything
should be done to strengthen them; which order
was cheerfully obeyed. During that night and on
the following day, when the artillery of the enemy
was silent, these trenches were placed in so good a
state of defence, that they offered perfect protection
to all within them.

At the same time one of the trenches was extended in the direction of the enemy's camp, which
caused them some annoyance, as they sent out
troops to prevent the work and report upon its progress. From this trench 800 Imperialists armed
with muskets sallied forth, and a skirmish ensued.
The enemy finding that the Imperialists were in the
open plain, sent three squadrons of cavalry aganst
them; but the Imperialists not only held their ground,

---

* Se disse que elles determinaram de cessar com a artilheria e
accommetter o arraial do Emperador; pode ser, que andaram melhor
em o não fazer, ao menos não se devem culpar por que o não fizeram.

but made so brilliant a charge, that the enemy was
routed and took to flight after great loss,* and they
then returned to the trench. Thus passed the
second day.

On the third day, at the same hour as before, the
enemy again opened their fire from their artillery;
but they did nothing more nor less than on the first
day. The men passing to and fro in the interior of
the camp were more exposed to danger than the
men in the trenches, and the Emperor's artillery did
more damage to the enemy on this day than on the
first. During the night false alarms were given
them, which gave them little rest. On the fourth
day they remained quiet, and nothing took place,
except the exchange of a few shots and some skirmishes. On the fifth day, dissatisfied and fatigued
from the trouble and work they had undergone, and
anxious, moreover, at the increasing extent of the
trench, knowing that it could not fail to cause them
great damage, they sent forward their heavy artillery
during the night, at the same hour upon which it
arrived on the first day, and they decamped on the
sixth. They withdrew with their squadrons in good
order, and marched to the camp, situated at two
leagues from Ingolstadt, where they had previously
established themselves. From thence they proceeded

---

* De sorte que rompendo se e abrindo se mostraram as costas, com
grande damno.

two leagues farther, and encamped at Neuburg, where they remained for some days. The Emperor meantime did not move from his camp, awaiting advices from Count de Buren, and from the troops he brought with him, so as to be able to regulate his line of action; for he was of the opinion that he had done enough with such inferior numbers, both as regards his entrenchment and the number of his troops by compelling the enemy, which had come to attack him with so much fury, to leave their positions and beat a retreat.*

Nearly at the same time the Emperor and the Protestants received the news that M. de Buren had operated the junction which he had been ordered to make, and that after having held a general inspection of his troops at the other side of the Rhine, he was advancing to cross that river to join His Majesty. The Protestants, who were daily and more exactly informed of the movements of M. de Buren,† had placed a large body of troops on the Rhine, on the Frankfort side, to prevent M. de Buren from crossing. The latter, however, displayed so much courage and activity, that he forced the passage in

---

* Por que lhe parecia, que tinha assaz feito de havendo táõ grande differença do seu campo e gente a dos enemigos que o vieram com tanta braveza accommetter, faser los deixar o seu alojamento o retirar se.

† Os Protestantes que mais particularmente e que cadia dia sabião.

spite of the enemy.* The Protestants on being informed of this left Neuburg, where they had their
camp, and took the direction of Bendingen, a domain
of the Duke of Bavaria, an excellent position for
an advance, and to close the road by which Count
Buren intended joining the Emperor. But as to
perform this march it would be necessary to leave at
a distance the principal towns of Suabia which, as
may be believed, were but little reassured at seeing
the Emperor and his army so close to them, they
altered their resolution, and returned to establish
themselves at Donauwerth, which they had left at
the onset. They would have done much better for
the success of their plan if they had returned to
Neuburg, where they were more capable of keeping
the Emperor at check than at Donauwerth. This
was the fourth and not the least mistake which they
committed.†

At this time the Emperor received the news that
Count de Buren had crossed the Rhine, and that he
was gradually advancing to form a junction with His
Majesty. He was also informed of the design of the
Protestants when they took the road to Bendingen;
and this caused him considerable anxiety, as he felt how
important it was that Count de Buren should arrive

* O qual contudo teve tanto esforço e pos tanta diligencia que
apezar delles e per força o passou.

† Che foi o quarto, e não menor erro, que commetteram.

without accident.* Consequently the Emperor resolved to advance on the rear of the Protestants, and
so to regulate his marches, and take up well fortified
positions, that the Protestants could not give battle
to the Count without being immediately obliged to
come to blows with His Majesty; and, should they
turn round against the Emperor, the Count would
find the road free and open to form his junction with
him.† The Count made such good speed that he
arrived with all his men safe and sound before Ingolstadt, at the Emperor's camp. The latter having
made in person a reconnaissance of the town of
Neuburg, crossed the Danube with his whole army,
near the camp, in front of Ingolstadt, and marched
against the said town of Neuburg, where there were
four bodies of infantry, which surrendered. The
Emperor left a garrison in Neuburg, and after having made all necessary arrangements, he encamped
in the Danube, at a place called Maresheim, a good
league from Donauwerth, where the enemy, as already
stated, had an entrenched camp, and where they had
been reinforced by the troops which they had left

---

* Visto quanto importava que o ditto conde viessa seguramente.

† Para o que o Emperador tinha determinado de indo nas costas
dos Protestantes fazer jornadas tão proporcionadas, e tomar sempre
alojamentos tão fortificados, que os Protestantes, não podessem pelejar
com o conde, que subito não ouvessem tambem de vir as maos com
Sua Magestade, ou, se virassam sobre Sua Magestade, o conde ficasse
o caminho livre e desembaraçado, para se poder vir ajuntar com Sua
Magestade.

in the rear to close the passage against M. de Buren; and although the camps were so close to each other during the few days passed in this position, no engagement took place.*

This induced the Emperor to hit upon another plan. He left his position at Maresheim, and leaving the Danube, upon which he had always held his camp, and leaving his enemies to the left, he reached a place in the Neuburg territory called Monheim. On the following day, which was the eve of St. Francis, starting from thence he went and established himself near a small mountain, situated opposite Ettingen and Nördlingen, upon which he placed a portion of his artillery, pitching his camp round it. Having done this, the Emperor at dusk was informed that the drums of the enemy were heard. The sound came from a wood which lay between the Emperor and the enemy; the darkness increased, and at the same time a mist arose: these various causes rendered it impossible to ascertain what the enemy was doing. The sound of drums was heard during the whole night, and during the morning of the following day, which was the festival of St. Francis. During the night the army and the Captain-General remained in camp to ascertain the movements and intentions of the army. The Em-

---

* Jamais se poderam morder.

peror, who two days previously had an attack of the
gout in the foot, was himself up during a greater
portion of the night, to receive any information that
might be acquired, and to give the necessary orders;
and though suffering great pain, he was up again
before daybreak. He confessed himself, and heard
mass, holding it for certain that on that day a
battle would be fought. Despite the mist and
despite the pain he experienced, he mounted on
horseback; and leaving the camp he rode up the
mountain upon which he had placed his artillery,
that he might sooner be informed of what was taking
place; but he suffered so much from the gout that
he was obliged to have a linen pad to his stirrup
to rest his foot, and he rode thus the whole day.*
All this time nothing could be ascertained respecting the enemy's movements, owing to the mist which
had arisen the preceding night, and which became
so dense that it was impossible to see two yards
before one as long as it lasted, and it did not clear
off till ten o'clock in the morning. It was then
ascertained that the enemy had passed through the
wood already mentioned, and that they occupied the
ridge of hills which stretch as far as Nördlingen,
upon which they had posted all their squadrons in
good order. It is true that the last of the rearguard

* Que for forçado por hum lençol sobrõ o arçáõ da sella em que
respousasse o pee, e assi o trouxe todo o dia.

I

and some others who were still in the ravine between
the wood and the mountain had to sustain such a
charge from the Imperial light horse, that they took
a much hastier movement than the ordinary step to
the mountains to join the main body of their army.[*]
In the interval the Emperor had ordered his whole
army to leave the camp. As soon as the fog had
cleared off, he drew up his squadrons in line of
battle; and having been advised that the enemy's
army was in sight, he advanced in good order and at
a measured step in the enemy's direction. He took
up his position on a small hill, which was nearer the
river, so as to be better able to see and give the
necessary orders. Here were assembled the Duke of
Alba his general, and many other captains and high
personages, discussing and saying each what he
thought most advisable. The Emperor, who owing
to his being so unwell, could not attend to work as
was his wont,[†] found that the majority of his captains were of the opinion that the river ought to be
crossed and battle given, or at least that a number of horsemen supported by infantry should be sent
across to charge the rearguard, and ascertain the
enemy's position, at the same time to keep the army
ready, as it was, to make a movement as soon as it

---

[*] Húa tal carga que elles se retiram mais que de passo para as
montanhas.
[†] Nem trabalhar como costumava fazer.

was necessary. As the Emperor, as already said, had not made a very careful study of the ground, and that all were agreed upon the necessity of giving battle, he adopted that opinion, and at once ordered the cavalry to cross the river. But whilst on the point of addressing his soldiers, to encourage them to advance to the battle, a better counsel was given him by one of the grandees of his house,* who explained to him the topography of the ground, and the impossibility of crossing the river to give battle, without running the evident and almost certain danger of defeat, owing to the great advantage which the enemies would have. The Emperor fully understood this, and immediately ordered the cavalry, which had already with some difficulty crossed the river, to be recalled; and it recrossed with still greater difficulty, as the passage was a very bad one; and the whole army returned to camp. As regards the enemy, they continued their march until they had established themselves on the high ground already spoken of, near Nördlingen.

Ought the river to have been crossed and battle given? On this point there was then, there has been since, and there are still to-day great discussions and divers opinions. The Emperor marched later to make a minute and careful examination of the

---

* Lhe foi dado outro parecer melhor de hum grande de sua casa.

ground, with no one to influence his opinion. The
result was that His Majesty, and all those who were
of the opinion that the river ought not to be crossed,
and that battle ought not to be given, were confirmed in their view, which ceased to be doubtful;
and the thing appeared to them the more impossible,
as it was far more easy for the enemy than for the
Emperor to have given battle. Those who on that
day had recommended battle, avowed, when they
had studied the ground, that their advice was worth-
less, and those who after the discussion expressed
their opinion that it would be wrong not to give
battle, confessed their mistake, also, as soon as they
had visited the ground. Those who have not seen it,
and who still maintain the opinion that battle ought
to have been given, would do well to visit the spot;
and should they still persist in their idea, it would
be advisable for them to represent to themselves
exactly the army which was on the other bank : * this
might probably modify their opinion.

As already said, the Emperor returned to sleep that
night in camp; but finding that the enemy were farther
off than he wished, he broke up the camp in the
morning, and pitched his tents on the banks of the
river, which the evening before had been the object of
so much discussion ; and it was then seen which advice
was the best. The camp included two small hills

---

* Faram bem d'imaginar o que exercito estara em contrario.

close to each other, and most favourably situated. When the Emperor took up these quarters, some Protestant horsemen came down from the mountains into the plain, and a body of Imperialists immediately crossed the river. A smart skirmish ensued, in which a number were killed on either side, but the loss of the Protestants was much more severe and important. Among others who fell was the Duke of Brunswick. However, it was already late, and the Emperor could not advance to support his men which the enemy could do, as he should have been obliged to cross the river. The Emperor, moreover, wished to fix his camp and ordered the skirmish to cease. At various times he examined, and ordered to be examined, different points, to see if there was any means of doing harm to the Protestants, but not finding any he secretly considered and weighed his plans; * at last he resolved to send the necessary number of troops to attack Donauwerth, an Imperial city, which the enemy had left when they advanced on Nördlingen, and where they had left a garrison entrusted with its defence. Consequently at nightfall he ordered the said troops to depart, who reached their destination at daybreak, and who at the first assault carried the outskirts. The city capitulated shortly afterwards.

---

* Cuidou e pratticou em segredo o que se poderia fazer.

CHAPTER VIII.

The Emperor crosses the River. — Surrender of Hastat. — Surrender
of Dillingen. — Surrender of Laubingen and Gondelfingen. —
Skirmish with the Enemy. — Crosses the Brenz and encamps at
Sontheim. — Lays an Ambuscade for the Protestants. — The Pro-
testant Position at Giengen. — The Papal Troops leave the Imperial
Camp. The Protestants wish to treat for Peace. — The Elector of
Saxony is defeated by Duke Maurice. — Dissensions in the
Protestant Army. — They raise their Camp and retire to Heyden-
heim. — The Imperial Army pursues them. — A Battle imminent.
Is prevented by a Snow-storm. — Surrender of Nördlingen and
other Towns. — The Protestants capture Gmündt. — Dispersion of
the Protestant Army. — John Frederick of Saxony retreats to
Gotha. — Surrender of Frankfort and of Ulm.

AFTER the surrender of Donauwerth, His Majesty
left his camp, and proceeded to that city with
the intention of following the Danube on the Ulm
side, to see if there were any means of cutting off
the enemy's supplies, and the hope of weakening
them and exhausting them (and the inhabitants
of the town of Ulm with them), by obliging them
to abandon the mountains and come to some spot
where it would be more easy to give them battle.*

It must be understood that, to go to Donauwerth,
the Emperor had necessarily to cross the river with
his army, and place himself in line in the open plain

* Onde mais facilmente che les podesse dar batalha.

near the Protestant camp. Although bridges of
boats had been established for crossing the river,
and although the fords were better known than when
they first arrived, the passage was nevertheless so
difficult (and there were still other rivers to cross on
the other side), that if the enemy had entertained
any great desire to fight, they might have done so on
that day with great advantage : * therefore, it may be
said, without knowing the motives that guided them,
that this may be counted as the fifth error which
they committed.†

The Emperor, finding that the Protestants would
not move, advanced in good order to the camp, which
was on the Danube, between Donauwerth and Hastat.
Those who occupied it abandoned it, and the inhabitants of Hastat brought the keys of their city to the
Emperor, who, on the following day, advanced on
Dillingen, which followed the example of Hastat.
He then established himself near Laubingen, a domain belonging to Duke Otho Henry of Bavaria,
where there were four German detachments, and,
that evening, they showed an intention of defending
themselves.

The Emperor, having been informed that the

* Que se os enemigos tiveram grande vontade de pelejar, elles o
poderam fazer neste dia com grande ventagem sua.

† Pelo que se pode julgar, sem saber as causas que a isto os
moveram, se posse esta contar pola quinta falta ou erro que elles
commetteram.

enemy wished to come to the support of this town,
and take up a position on some high ground at the
verge of a forest, ordered, although some distance
from the town, that on the following day at daybreak the whole army should hold itself ready to
advance on whatever point he might think it advisable. He started himself early with the Duke of
Alba, his general, and many of his council, to ascertain which would be the most advantageous position
to assume to attack the enemy as they emerged from
the said forest. Whilst on his way, some of the
inhabitants of the town came and surrendered it
to His Majesty. The inhabitants of Gondelfingen
did the same. Those of Laubingen informed him
that the four detachments had withdrawn, and crossed
the bridge over the Danube before daylight, with
some pieces of artillery, and with one of the captains
of the League who had arrived there the evening
before, and had prevented them surrendering at once;
and they added, that with those four detachments
and artillery they had taken the Augsburg road.

On the receipt of this news, the Emperor, observing that he was not aware of any movement having
taken place in the Protestants' camp, rejoined the
army, and passing by Laubingen, in which town he
left a sufficient garrison, he ordered some light-horse
to cross the river in pursuit of the said four detachments. They came up with them, and, after a skirmish,

pressed them so closely that they abandoned their
artillery, which was brought to the Emperor. In his
eagerness to advance, the Emperor marched so rapidly, that on the same day he crossed the river Brenz,
and pitched his camp at Sontheim, a town situated
on the bank of another river, which runs towards
Ulm. On arriving there, the Emperor was informed
that some of the enemy's horse was in the vicinity,
in a small Imperial town named Giengen, on the
said river Brenz. His Majesty sent his General there
with a suitable force, but as soon as the horsemen
perceived him they beat a retreat. Some of the
enemy's gendarmes were in the same town: these
latter, hoping or knowing that their whole army
would arrive on the following day, dissimulated, as
it was already late when they were summoned to
surrender, giving their word that they would surrender on the morrow, and thus gained a night by their
deceit. That same night, the Emperor having come
to the camp, he sent out spies in various directions
to learn something of the enemy's movements. Some
came back without any news, and others were made
prisoners by the enemy's videttes. The Emperor
was consequently irresolute and undecided how to
act in the morning; he did not know whether it would
not be better to take the direction of Ulm and steal
a march upon the enemy, or stop where he was,
because, by making haste, they might also have

taken up a position which would have cut off his supplies.

The Emperor, being in this doubt, received the news that the Protestants were on their march; but he did not yet know where they wished to establish themselves. Consequently the Emperor and his General and many other personages went to reconnoitre the movements of the enemy, who were advancing in good order to take up a position at Giengen. The Emperor, not having placed his army in order of battle, on the contrary, being ready to march on the opposite bank to that occupied by the enemy towards Ulm, returned to the camp and ordered his troops back to their quarters; the enemy did the same.

The Emperor, having ascertained the position and plans of the enemy, resolved that day to lay a good ambuscade for them, but it was not well carried out.

It is presumed, however, that, had it been so, it would have been attended with good results; for, despite the carelessness with which it was done, the Imperial musketeers did so much havoc among the enemy that they always remembered that day. In fact, whenever afterwards the Emperor wished to lay an ambuscade, such as it ought to be, taking advantage of a favourable opportunity, and sending out skirmishers to attack the enemy, it was never possible to induce any number of them to go far from the

camp. The failure of the ambuscade is perhaps also
to be attributed to the fact that Giengen is situated
in a hollow, and the Protestants had their camp on
the banks of the river, on the side opposite to that
upon which His Majesty had his. On this side of His
Majesty's camp there was a mound, which dominated
Giengen as well as the Protestant camp. The latter
therefore crossed the river, and took possession of
that mound with a considerable force; and as it
was difficult to come to their support from one camp
to the other, they entrenched themselves strongly in
that position, and from their encampment they
discovered a portion of the ambuscade which had
been laid. The result was that His Majesty ordered
the troops employed in it to return to camp. With
a view to try every means to annoy the enemy, a
night assault was resolved upon; but the enemy
were on the alert, and took their precautions so well,
that it was wisely given up. As the Protestants
occupied the mound already mentioned above Giengen, on the same side of the river as the Imperial
camp, and as His Majesty occupied another mound
in the same manner, on the side where the Protestant quarters were, for many reasons, as soon as
they arrived at Giengen, it was resolved to fortify
the mound which was opposite the Imperial camp,
to lodge the Italians there who had remained: for
most of them had left, complaining of bad treatment

and bad pay. Those who remained were disaffected,
so much so that when the Pope's Legate left, having
been recalled by His Holiness, they endeavoured to
seize upon the opportunity of returning to their
country, at the very moment when it was desirable
to increase the numerical strength of His Majesty's
army, because the Protestants were receiving numerous reinforcements from Würtemberg, and were
placing a garrison in a fort under construction.
Out of the 4,000 men belonging to His Holiness,
3,000 one morning took their departure. The Emperor
was thus frustrated in his plans,* as he had not sufficient troops left to garrison the fort which he had commenced, and which consequently was left unfinished.

The season was already far advanced, as it was
near the festival of All Saints, and the rains had
commenced. The Emperor, finding that from his
camp he could do no harm to the enemy, resolved,
after some petty skirmishes, to recross the river and
take up his quarters near Laubingen. He therefore
broke up his camp and advanced in good order,
expecting the enemy to try their fortune, which,
according to some, they might have and ought to
have done.† However, from good reasons of their
own, they did not move on that day, and the

---

* Ficou frustrado de seu intento.

† Se os nemigos quereriam tentar a fortuna, o que algús querem
que elles poderam e deveram fazer.

Emperor continued to march to the spot where he wished to establish himself. The rain and bad weather continued. Moreover, the ground was heavy and damp, and the Imperial camp full of mud. Although the enemy's camp was on the heights, it was not, as was learnt afterwards, in a better condition.* This explains why, the whole time the Emperor was in camp, nothing of importance was achieved. On the contrary, at the same period the Protestants wished to treat for peace; but His Majesty, finding that no suitable agreement could be come to, broke off the negotiations. Whilst His Majesty was at the said camp, he received the news that John Frederick of Saxony had been defeated by the troops of the King and of Duke Maurice.

In consequence of the inclemency of the weather, and from other reasons which actuated some persons, it was the general opinion that the Emperor ought to place his troops in garrison. In this manner he would have closely pressed the Protestants, especially the towns held by them, for these garrisons would have cut off all their provisions and supplies, and thus harassed them considerably; but the Emperor considered that the whole good effect of his enterprise consisted in dispersing the army of the Protestants, and in separating their forces: he fancied

---

* Não ficaram de melhor condição.

that placing his army in garrisons was to divide, weaken, and break it up.* The Emperor repeatedly had quarters examined which appeared advantageous and suitable for wintering and keeping the enemy at bay, until it was seen which of the two armies would be the first to relinquish the struggle or obliged to disband itself.† He then left the above-mentioned locality, because it was damp and muddy, and consequently not very agreeable or advantageous for an army; and he looked out for another position free from humidity, strong, and well situated to suit and satisfy his soldiers.‡ It has been maintained that on that day the Protestants might again have given battle with advantage.§ If that was the case, and if they committed an error, the fault must rest with him who committed it.|| His Majesty resolved therefore to carry out his enterprise to the end, and to persevere until one of the two armies should be obliged to disband, either by compulsion, bad weather, famine, or any other calamity.¶

* Mas considerando Sua Magestade que todo o bom effeito de sua empresa consistia em romper o exercito e dividir as forças dos protestantes, pareceo che que per o seu em garnições seria dividilo, diminuilo e rompelo.

† Atee ver qual dos dous exercitos se dexixaria primeiro, ou seria forçado a se desfazer.

‡ Paro outro enxuto, forte, de bello assento, e agosto e satisfaçaõ dos soldados.

§ Querem dizer.

|| Se assi lie e se commeteram erro, se deve deixar ao que nisso ha.

¶ Sua Magestade determinou seguir sua empresa atee o fim e

The Emperor was informed that there was another spot in an excellent situation, where he might, by keeping close to the enemy, cause them some damage, and acquire such an advantage over them as to compel them to break up and separate; * and he resolved to carry out this enterprise within a brief delay. But as the matter was one of high importance and not without its difficulties, and as no one ought to undertake an arduous and perilous enterprise without the necessary preparations, the Emperor put off its execution to an opportune moment. Now, it so happened that at the same time the town of Nördlingen offered to surrender, and the Emperor thought that, by occupying it, he should find another means of annoying the enemy, leaving it optional to adopt and take either measure. The Emperor admitted the good position and the great advantages of this locality, and endeavoured to turn it to account to overthrow his enemy. Like others, who also afterwards examined it, he deemed that it was feasible and practicable, provided that it was well executed.

The Protestants thought that the march of the Emperor on Laubingen was the result of some necessity or discouragement; † but on finding that

---

persistir atee que hum dos dous exercitos fosse per força, por ruim tempo, per fame, ou por outra qualquer necessidade constrangido a se desfazer.

* Que por força os levaria debaixo, e faria romper e dividir.

† Procedera de algua necessidade ou desfallecimento.

the Emperor occupied the quarters above indicated,
they found themselves deceived in their hopes. Thus,
when they learnt that His Majesty was again approaching them, they displayed much less energy
and courage than formerly,* and, despite the skirmishes opened by the Emperor, and the opportunities
he offered them to leave their camp, there was no
means of inducing them to do so.† Already differences and disputes had arisen amongst them; the
Imperial cities were weary of the heavy sums levied
upon them, and the other members of the League
could not provide them.‡ Consequently the Protestants sent away their heavy artillery; and finally,
on the morning of November 22, wearied and
worn by labour, bad weather, and by many other
annoyances, and from other motives which they knew
better than anyone else, they raised their camp and
withdrew to the mountains at the other side of the
Brenz, under the protection of a castle situated on
the frontier of Würtemberg, called Heydenheim.

On the preceding night, the Emperor had been
informed by a spy that the heavy artillery of the
Protestants had left; and, fearing what actually did

* Mostroram logo muito menos spiritos e coragem do que d'antes
tinham.

† Não ouve remedio para os tira fora.

‡ E tendo ja passado entrelles algúas contradiçoes e disputas, e
enfadando se as cidades imperiaes dos grandes gastos e despesas que
faziam, e não podendo os outros da liga supprir os gastos.

occur, he sent back the same spy to the enemy's camp with orders to return, no matter at what hour, and report what they were doing. This spy, who left at midnight to give the information, related that at that hour they were on the move, but as he had met troops on his road, he was obliged to turn back, and, owing to the darkness of the night, and the fog, he had lost his way; so that he did not reach the Emperor's camp until His Majesty had left it. Whether he told the truth, or whether these were only false excuses, the result was that he returned very late, and not in time to be of any service; for the Emperor, having been informed about ten o'clock in the morning that the Protestants, as stated, had left, at once sent his General with a small body of horse and musketeers to ascertain the truth.* His Majesty followed him with other knights, leaving orders for the whole of the cavalry to advance promptly, and for the whole of the infantry to be prepared to act at a moment's notice. Having passed the camp abandoned by the Protestants, they were pursued, until one of their squadrons,† which served as a rear-guard, was come upon, with which a skirmish ensued, so that all their army formed in line of battle, and commenced to march

---

* Cum algús cavallos, e arcabuzeiros desmandados.

† Assi despois de ter atravessado o seu campo, os protestantes dos atee foram segui se ver hum dos seus esquadrões.

K

to sustain the struggle.* After some discussion as
to what ought to be done, the Emperor ordered all
the cavalry to stop where it was, in view of the
enemy; and as it was already late, he returned immediately to his camp to order the infantry and the
artillery to advance, as his intention was to establish
that very night his whole army so close to the
enemy that he could attack them at daybreak. The
infantry and artillery immediately began to advance,
following His Majesty, who served as a guide,† and
they arrived, one hour after midnight, where the main
body of the troops were quartered, and where they
rested, each man as best he could, according to time
and place, without leaving his detachment the remainder of the night.

The Emperor had proceeded forward to rejoin
his General closer to the enemy; but when the day
broke upon which he hoped to carry out his designs,
a heavy fall of snow succeeded the severe cold of the
preceding night, and the Emperor, seeing that his
soldiers, having only their arms with them, had
nothing to protect them from the cold and from
hunger,‡ resolved to return to the camp which he
had left the evening before: and it is well he did

---

* E começou a caminhar para ter mão, e sostentar a escaramuça.
† Seguendo a Sua Magestade que servia di guia.
‡ Vendo que os soldados não tinham outro reparo contra o fomes e o
frio que suas armas.

so, as the Protestants were so well posted that, had
it been the finest weather in the world, nothing could
have been attempted against them with any success.

The Emperor, on his return to camp, did not remain
there long, but immediately advanced to prevent
the Protestants gaining some strong and favourable
position;* for at this moment they sought for support
in the strength and situation of the ground, and were
in the midst of mountains, and in steep and difficult
paths. This induced the inhabitants of Nördlingen,
and of other towns and castles where they had left
troops, and who saw themselves abandoned without
hope of help, to submit to His Majesty. The Emperor, whose object was rather to scatter and dis-
unite the Protestants than to take vengeance on the
said places,† accepted their submission, and took the
road to Nördlingen.

As already said, the winter had set in severely.
The soldiers were fatigued and worn out, and the
majority, or nearly all, were of the opinion that it
would be well if the Emperor remained satisfied with
the results obtained, and were to place his troops to
garrison on the frontier and allow his army to repose. The Emperor would willingly have done so,
as well to spare his troops, as not to appear to follow

---

* Que não tornassem para a terra bea o grossa.

† Cuja tenção sendo mais accobar de romper e dividir a os protestantes, que tomar vingança dos dittos lugares.

only his own counsel;* but he foresaw to what inconveniences it would lead, and thus the fruit would
be lost of all the successes already obtained, for the
Protestants had agreed between themselves that they
would go with their whole army, and take up their
quarters in Franconia, to reprovide themselves with
money, men, and supplies, so as to recommence the
struggle with renewed obstinacy. He therefore resolved, much against his will, to follow his own
opinion.† To this must be added the important
consideration, that he had some reason to hope that
if the two armies continued on the road which they
were following — the one always in the track of the
other, at a distance of four, five, or six leagues —
an opportunity might offer itself, by approaching
the enemy as near as possible, and by marching
during a whole night, the nights being long, of attacking them at daybreak. His Majesty therefore
started, following the road to the right through a
good country, in the direction of Dingelspuhel. That
town had also joined the League, and, although it
held out a long time before it returned to its duty,
it at last surrendered. The Emperor then advanced
on Rotenburg, which had not joined the League,
and which also sent a deputation to meet His
Majesty. The Protestants marched through a moun-

---

* Como por não seguir quasi soo opinião.
† Se determinou bem contra sua vontade de seguir sua opinião.

tainous country, making circuits and returning on their steps, so that they had to endure much more fatigue and embarrassment than the Imperial army. To show that they were doing something, they attacked and captured Gmündt, an Imperial town, which had always remained faithful, and which still adhered to the ancient religion; therefore the Emperor afterwards indemnified it handsomely for all that it had suffered, at the cost of those who had been the cause thereof.

The Protestants found that, by the plan adopted by the Emperor, their own projects were disconcerted, and that they were obliged to separate and dissolve,* as on the road which it was following the army of the Emperor did not deviate from the direction indicated above. The Protestants daily dispersed, leaving behind a portion of their artillery and baggage, so that in a short time their army was completely broken up. All that remained consisted of a small body of troops under John Frederick of Saxony, who, through a woody and mountainous country, succeeded in crossing the Maine, and sought refuge at Gotha, a stronghold in his estates. The Emperor, the better to ascertain what was actually taking place, sent on Count de Buren with the men that remained under his

---

* Ficavam frustrados de seus intentos e constrangidos a se romper ou dividir.

orders from Rotenburg, and he did not meet with
the same obstacles which he had to contend against
on his arrival. Already the Imperial city of Frankfort had announced that it submitted to the Emperor,
and, after having received a garrison, it sent deputies
to perform the act of submission. This having been
done, the Emperor, finding that he did not meet with
any further resistance, and that, on the contrary,
many towns which had been hostile to him commenced to treat for their submission, halted a few
days at Rotenburg, where he placed his soldiers
under cover, and allowed them some repose. Here
he had an attack of the gout; but as soon as he felt
a little better, and the army had rested and restored
itself, he advanced towards the town of Halle, in
Suabia (which had joined the League, but which
recognised its error), where he had another attack
of gout. In this town the Elector came to greet him,
regretting that he had not done better.* The inhabitants of Ulm also returned to obedience, avowing
their fault. A garrison was placed in the city.

* O Elector veo alli fazer a reverencia, bem pezaroso de o não ter
feito melhor.

CHAPTER IX.

The Emperor enters Würtemberg. — Augsburg and Strasburg surrender. — Death of the King of England. — The Elector of Saxony reassembles an Army.—Pope Paul recalls his Italian auxiliaries. — Defeat of the Imperialists under Margrave Albert of Brandenburg. — Death of the Queen of the Romans. — The Emperor is taken seriously ill at Nördlingen. — Death of the King of France. — The Protestants encamp near Meissen on the Elbe. — Surrender of Meissen to the Imperialists. — The Protestants take up a position at Mühlberg. — The Emperor resolves to give Battle. — A dense Mist conceals his Movements. — The Protestants are taken by surprise and commence retreating. — The Imperialists cross the River. — Commencement of the Battle. — The Emperor attacks the Protestant Army with Cavalry only. — Duke Maurice defeats the Protestant Horse. — Total Defeat of the Protestants.— Capture of Duke John Frederick of Saxony, and of Duke Ernest of Brunswick, April 24.

THE Emperor, having somewhat recovered from the gout, started for Heilbron, a town which had also joined the League, and which had acted like most of the others, and he sent forward his General into the state of Würtemberg. As soon as he had entered it, in a few days all the towns in the plain surrendered to him. The Duke of that state sent a deputation to enter into negotiations, and, after an exchange of propositions and replies, an arrangement was concluded, and the Duke was received by the Emperor, to whom he did obedience. The Emperor was again tormented by the gout at Heilbron; and it lasted

so long that, even when he left for Ulm, where he arrived early in the year 1547, he had not yet recovered
his health. As happened in his previous attack, he
had continued relapses; so that this may be considered
his thirteenth attack of gout. At last he resolved
to master it by strict adherence to treatment and
diet. Meantime the inhabitants of Augsburg, also
admitting their error, waited upon His Majesty, and
tendered their obedience. A garrison was sent also to
their city. The inhabitants of Strasburg followed their
example. The news of the death of the King of
England reached His Majesty about the same time.

1547   Whilst the Emperor, as already said, was at Ulm,
where he was awaiting the fine season, to place himself under a regular system, and assure his convalescence,* each day brought him news after news
that John Frederick of Saxony (who, it will be remembered, had only preserved with him a small body
of troops from the great Protestant army, with which
he had retired to Gotha) was reinforcing himself
and constantly increasing the number of his men.
Not only did he wish to attempt to reconquer what
the King of the Romans and Duke Maurice had
deprived him of, but moreover he was exerting himself, and making preparations to seize upon their possessions, to excite and agitate their subjects, and to

---

* Esperando sazão arromodada para se por em regimento, e se
curar para o effeito e fim.

do them as much harm as he possibly could.* The King of the Romans and Duke Maurice kept His Majesty daily informed of what was taking place; and it was agreed that a portion of the army which remained with the Emperor, which, from the fatigues it had undergone, was considerably diminished, should be sent in that direction; what had still more contributed to reduce it was, that it happened precisely at this time that Pope Paul (in addition to all the bad acts he had done, as in part already related, and which he afterwards did by writing certain things to the Swiss, which he thought would be very prejudicial to the Emperor†) charged his Nuncio to inform His Majesty that he recalled all the Italian soldiers whom he had hitherto paid. Despite all the Emperor's entreaties that he would not do so, and that he would associate himself to the honour of victory,‡ the Pope would not hearken to him, and the said Italians withdrew.

The Emperor therefore found himself much put out § on finding that, on the one hand, it was difficult to separate his troops, and on the other that his

---

* Trabalhava e procurava de tomar o seu delles, e concitar e alterar seus subditos e em fim de lhes fazer o peor que podesse.

† Alem de todos os officios que o Papa Paulo tinha feitos como em parte acima se contem, e despois fez escrevendo aos Suiços algúa cousa, que cuidava ser de grande prejuizo.

‡ Por mais que o Emperador instou que tal não fizesse e que quisesse ter parte na honra da victoria.

§ Confuso.

health required careful treatment,* and he did not
know what to decide upon. However, seeing the
success of John Frederick, and, later, the defeat and
the captivity of the Margrave Albert of Brandenburg,
who had been sent by the Emperor with a body of
horse and foot to the support of the King his
brother, and of Duke Maurice; having at the same
time learnt the death of the Queen of the Romans,
his sister-in-law, and considering the sorrow and
affliction which the King her husband felt at it, he
resolved (as much to console him as to assist him †)
to adjourn the treatment and diet which the state of
his health required. He therefore deemed it advisable to leave at Augsburg, at Ulm, and at Frankfort, the garrisons which he had placed there, and
left at once with the rest of his army; and as not
only was it not advisable to divide it, but, on the
contrary, it was necessary to increase it, he raised a
new regiment of Germans. Having done this he
took his departure from Ulm, and, on reaching
Nördlingen, he was taken so ill from all the suffering and fatigue which he had undergone, that he was
compelled to remain some days there. However,
seeing the inconveniences which might result from
too long a delay, he started again, as best he could,
carried in a litter,‡ and continued his journey to

* Que sua saüde pedia cura.
† Assi polo consolar em hum caso, como polo adjudar em outro.
‡ Em liteira e couse pode.

Nüremberg, where he was received as in a city which
had not taken part in the League, and which had
never been hostile to him. Here he had a relapse,
so that he was obliged to remain there longer than
he wished. However, he made such an effort * that,
sometimes in a litter, sometimes otherwise, he reached
Egra. During this journey he met with the King
his brother and Duke Maurice, and the son of the
Elector of Brandenburg. The latter, from the
affection his house had always shown towards that
of Austria, and leaving all questions of opinion aside,†
had agreed with the King of the Romans to provide
him with troops, and to assist him in this war, which,
as has been said, was not engaged only with Duke John
Frederick, but which had disturbed to such a point the
populations of Bohemia, that they wished to partici-
pate in it more than became them.‡ Whilst their
Majesties were at Egra, they received the news of
the death of the King of France. They so settled
their affairs that, a few days afterwards, they left
with all their troops. The Emperor had previously
issued orders to the Duke of Alba, his general, and
to other captains, to remove certain obstacles which
might delay the march: they performed their duty

* Contudo se esforcou e fez tanto.

† Segundo a affeição que sua casa tirera sempre a de Austria,
deixando todas as opinioés suspensas.

‡ Mas tambem elle tinha de tal modo concitado aos de Boemia que
si quiseram metter mais nella do que lhes estava bem.

so well that they subjected all the towns and places of the opposite party which were on their passage, and the garrisons which occupied them were routed and their colours taken from them. Their Majesties left on the day following, so that after nine days they reached Somhof, a property belonging to Duke Maurice. As soon as they arrived there, Duke Maurice and the Duke of Alba went to reconnoitre the lower part of the river to see what ought to be done. On their return, after some reports and some false alarms, they acquired the certain information that Duke John Frederick had his camp at Meissen, on the other bank of the Elbe, at three good leagues from the spot mentioned above, where their Majesties were staying. As the soldiers had marched during these nine days almost without stopping, the Emperor thought it as well that they should repose the day after their arrival, as an opportunity might offer itself, which in fact was the case, of striking a blow.* During this day of repose given to the army, the Emperor, not to remain idle, and to be informed of the enemy's movements, sent out reconnaissances on two sides. One party went straight to Meissen, where they did not see the enemy's camp, because, as they convinced themselves, they had decamped during the night. That town sur-

* De fazer algun bom negocio.

rendered, but they found the bridge broken and
burnt. The other party, who had gone up the river,*
discovered the enemy's army in march on the other
bank of the river; and about three o'clock in the
afternoon they saw the advanced guard establish
itself on a spot on the left bank of the Elbe, called
Mühlberg, at three leagues from the camp of their
Majesties; and they judged from the baggage that accompanied it that the rear-guard could not take up its
quarters before midnight. This various information
reached the Emperor almost at the same time, about
five o'clock in the afternoon; and God knows how
sorry he was at having stopped that day, as it appeared to him that the following day would be too
late to reach the enemy; but God in his goodness
willed that it should be so.†

The Emperor calculated that the army of the
Protestants had marched nearly twenty-four hours,
and that it was impossible for them to dislodge at
once and do a long day's march; he had also been
informed the day he arrived at Somhof that there
were one or two fords near or opposite Mühlberg,
where the river was passable, though broad and deep.
He therefore sent without delay for the King his

---

* Os que foram contra a corrente do rio.

† Deus sabe se se arrependeo bem de se ter detido aquelle dia, por
que lhe parecia, que nao haveria tempo ao outro dia para poder
alcançar aos enemigos, o que todavia Deus por sua bontade remediou.

brother and Duke Maurice, to whom, as also to his
General, he communicated what his ideas and plans
were.*   Although he met with opposition from some,
especially because they did not believe there was
any ford, his opinion was nevertheless approved by
the others, and prevailed. To compensate for and
repair the fault which he thought he had committed
by not starting on that day, he wished to leave at
once at that very hour with his whole army, leaving
behind the invalids and baggage; but he found
opponents,† because the camp was surrounded by a
rivulet and difficult to be got out of, so that, as it was
already night, an exit from the camp could not be
done without much confusion and disorder. The
Emperor giving in to this opinion, seeing that it was
reasonable, resolved to postpone the departure till
the morning. And so as not to be wanting in anything of which he might stand in need, he ordered
his General to take along with him some pieces of
light artillery from the camp, and all the boat and
pontoon carriages. In fact, should one of the fords
not be practicable, he wished to throw over a bridge
of boats to send promptly across a sufficient body
of infantry to support the cavalry, which was to cross
by the other ford; and should that not answer, he
resolved at last to attempt (by crossing the river

---

* O que tinha no pensamento e vontade de fazer.
† Mas foi lhe isto contrariado.

somehow or other) every means to inflict as much
damage and do as much harm as possible to the
Protestants.

Having adopted this resolution, and everything
which ought to be done during the night having
been performed, the Emperor retired to rest till
midnight. He then got up and gave the signal to
saddle,* so that everything might be ready for marching at daybreak. Before dawn he sent forward the
Duke of Alba with some light horse and mounted
musketeers to reconnoitre the enemy's movements
and position. The Emperor, after having heard
mass with the King his brother and Duke Maurice,
followed him with the advanced guard, and, having
set his whole army, or at least the greater portion of
it, in movement, as was required, he commenced
the march at the first rays of dawn (which at this
season breaks about three o'clock in the morning),
and at eight o'clock in the morning took up a position opposite the enemy's camp.

During the whole of that morning there was a
dense mist, which was a great obstacle to the march,
and the Emperor was much annoyed at the em-
barrassments and delays which under these circumstances the fog occasioned him. The fog still
prevailed when they arrived opposite the enemy's

* E logo fez dar sinal a *cellare*.

camp, so that nothing could be discerned. However,
the Emperor placed everything in the hands of
God, that, whether he should be preserved or perish,
His will should be done,* and God in His mercy
deigned all of a sudden to clear away the fog, and
give such a clear sky, that it was discovered that the
supposition which His Majesty had made on the
previous day had been realised; for not only had
the enemy not taken their departure, nor were they
making any show of moving, but they were not
aware of the arrival of their Majesties with an army;
and, moreover, the fog which had impeded the march
of their Majesties was favourable to them by preventing the enemy discovering the Imperial army
up to this moment, which, despite the fog, had advanced in such good order that every man was in
the rank allotted to him.

Their Majesties and Duke Maurice proceeded in
advance to examine the resources and the nature of
the ground. The Emperor's General brought him
a report of his observations, still maintaining his
doubts as to the existence of a ford. Consequently,
their Majesties took the direction of a small village
in the vicinity, to find some one to point them out
the ford, and they succeeded so well that they met
a young peasant on an ass, who had crossed it the

* Contudo pondo o Emperador tudo nas mãos de Deus para que
se os quisesse conserva ou arruinar, sua vontade fosse feita.

preceding night, and offered to point it out to them. Their Majesties sent him on to the General; and whilst their Majesties and Duke Maurice were eating a mouthful,* they sent forward a strong body of matchlock-men to open the ball as soon as the fog cleared.†

As soon as the fog cleared off the enemy discovered what they had not yet seen; for they fancied that the troops which had arrived at the bank of the stream they had seen were not more numerous than those which they had seen the evening before, and of which they made no account. But as soon as they recognised what they had by no means expected, they immediately commenced taking down their tents and flags, mounting their horses, and placing themselves in marching order. They moreover sent their pontoon boats down the river in the direction of Torgau and Wittenberg, towns which belonged to John Frederick of Saxony, thinking thereby to save them.

Their Majesties had already left the village, where they had breakfasted, to give the necessary orders. Some Hungarians, light horse, and mounted musketeers, were ordered in all haste opposite Torgau; and when they arrived there a skirmish ensued, in which the troops at Torgau sent them some volleys

* Temiam hum bocado.
† Paraque, tanto que a nevoa caisse, começassem a festa.

of artillery. During their march their Majesties
were informed of what was taking place, and of the
measures taken to save the boats. The Emperor
then ordered his General to throw forward the
above-mentioned musketeers, whom His Majesty
met; they at once returned towards the river, some
of them wading into it, and opened fire. The
enemy, despite the resistance they made with their
artillery and musketry, were compelled to abandon
their boats, and some Spanish musketeers, who had
swam across the river with their swords between
their teeth, brought them to their Majesties on the
bank. Meantime a portion of the enemy's army had
commenced leaving the banks of the river: this
allowed the young peasant above-mentioned to point
out the ford. The Emperor immediately ordered
the Hungarians, some light horse, and the musketeers,
to attempt the passage, which they did bravely.
Finally, after a double volley on either side, the
enemy deemed it prudent to leave the river, and this
was doubtless the sixth error which they committed.*
For had they made a stand and attempted to defend
the river, it would have been impossible on that day
to have found the ford or to dislodge them, and the
night would have enabled them to place themselves

---

* Esta se pode bem contar, e sem duvida ter pola sua sexta falta
e erro.

in safety. They must know best what induced them to do this.*

The enemy having abandoned the river to the Emperor, he was eagerly entreated to allow the cavalry to cross and pursue them. But, considering that it was by his determination and advice that the army had been led there, he replied that he had not acted thus to receive an insult, but rather, with God's blessing, he hoped to obtain the honour of victory.†
He held this language because the enemy was as strong as he was in cavalry, and had moreover five to six thousand infantry with artillery, which His Majesty could not have so promptly at hand, as a little time was requisite to throw over the bridge, which was too short for so broad a river; and whilst this was being done, the Emperor sent one of the principal personages of the army ‡ to the other bank, with the express order to inform him as soon as the enemy was a short league distant from the river. For he was convinced (taking into consideration the impediments occasioned to their march by the Hungarians and the light horse) that that distance was not too great, after effecting the passage, to come up with them. If, on the contrary, they

* Elles devem saber o que os moveo a fazer isto.
† Mas considerando que por sua determinaçáõ e parecer tinha la levado o exercito, respondeo que não fizera isto para receber affronta, antes entendia com o favor de Deus alcançar a honra da victoria.
‡ Algúa pessoa principal.

wished to make a stand against the Emperor, the
bridge was already so far advanced, and such dili-
gence had been shown, that infantry and artillery
were ready to sustain the combat.

As soon as the Emperor received the information
he was waiting for, he immediately ordered all the
Hungarians and light horse to advance with the
whole of the vanguard, with which was Duke Maurice,
and which was commanded by the Duke of Alba.
Their Majesties having left sufficient troops to
guard the camp, followed them immediately with
the main body, and they made such good speed that,
after three German leagues, they came up with them.
Although some thought it hazardous to attack with
cavalry only, without infantry and artillery, as the
enemy was strongly entrenched in a position near a
swamp, the Emperor considered, nevertheless, that
it was already late, and that it was impossible, after
the distance they had gone, for the infantry and
artillery to follow up. He considered also that it
was important to put an end to this war, and that,
if the enemy escaped this time, it might be continued
longer than it ought. He moreover discovered a certain fear amongst the enemy,* and he saw by their
movements that they were disconcerted and taken
by surprise;† he therefore resolved to do his best

* Certo pavor.
† Como attonitos e pasmados.

with the cavalry he had with him. Consequently he ordered his General to advance and reconnoitre the enemy's position and movements. The latter found them such that at the entrance of a wood (where their infantry were posted in good order with some artillery) he charged with Duke Maurice and the vanguard. The enemy's horse were broken, and carried disorder among the infantry, and those who escaped took to flight. As, owing to the swamp, their Majesties could not keep the main body in that order which they had maintained in the open country, they were obliged to follow the vanguard, which they did to keep up the habitual order, and to serve as a reinforcement and support if required. The enemy was pursued for nearly a good German mile; and when their Majesties pulled up, they were informed that Duke John Frederick had been taken prisoner. The Duke of Alba having returned from the pursuit (it lasted the whole night and a portion of the following day), the Emperor charged him to seek out John Frederick, and the Duke of Alba brought him and presented him. The Emperor entrusted him to the watchful custody of the said Duke, with an escort of soldiers sufficient to guard him in safety. Duke Ernest of Brunswick was also brought as a prisoner to His Majesty, and handed over to the same custody. These orders having been given, their Majesties, with the troops which they could reassemble, and which were returning from the pursuit, started on their return to the camp, which was on the other side of the river, and on their way they met the infantry and light artillery, which had followed them as rapidly as was possible. They were entrusted with the care of the chariots and baggage which had remained on the road, and after having marched three more good German leagues, the bridge was crossed, and the camp reached about midnight. This occurred on April 24.

CHAPTER X.

Siege of Wittenberg. — The Town capitulates. — Surrender of other Towns. — Duke Maurice is appointed Elector. — War in Bohemia. — Convocation of a Diet. — Submission of the Elector of Saxony and of the Landgrave of Hesse. — Mutiny amongst the Imperial Troops. — Disturbances in Italy. — Conspiracy of Fiesco. — The States of the Empire submit to the Council. — Revolution at Placentia. — Charles's Nephew is appointed King of Bohemia. — The Emperor returns to the Netherlands.

THEIR Majesties remained two days in the camp. On the third day they left for Torgau, which at once threw open its gates to the Emperor. During the march, all the flags and standards taken in the battle were presented to him. Their Majesties continuing their march, pitched their camp opposite Wittenberg, where they received the news of the defeat, near Bremen, of Duke Henry of Brunswick. The siege of Wittenberg took place in the usual manner. The Elector Margrave of Brandenburg proceeded to the Emperor, and negotiations were commenced for an arrangement, as well on the part of John Frederick of Saxony, as on that of his wife and children, who were inside the town; and the result of these negotiations was, that the town capitulated. Other towns also surrendered, others were demolished, all accord-

ing to what had been agreed upon; and, according
to the same conventions, the said Duke continued to
remain guarded at the Court of His Majesty, who
gave the title of Elector, and the appointments
belonging to it, to Duke Maurice, for the good services which he had rendered him, and for the good-
will and affection he entertained and showed towards
him.* The Emperor ordered to be set at liberty
the Marquis Albert of Brandenburg and Duke Henry
of Brunswick, and others who had been made prisoners previously.

The King of the Romans and the Elector, Duke
Maurice, with the troops which they had brought
with them, left Wittenberg two days before the
Emperor's departure; the King to put down the
disturbances in Bohemia, and the Duke to put his
affairs into order, according to what had been agreed
upon by common accord.†

The Emperor, considering that it was a long time
that he had been carrying on these two wars, and
that there did not remain any leader of importance
who could take the field against him, resolved to
disband his troops, and wished to terminate what
remained to be done by friendly measures, and by

---

* Polas bonos servicos, que lhe fizera e boa vontade e affeicam, que
lhe tinha e mostrava.

† Por seguvar suas cousas conforme as que entre todos estava concertado.

a general conference of the Deputies of the Empire. He resolved upon the convocation of a Diet, and for that purpose he left for Halle in Saxony, where he was received with complete obedience. During this journey a deputation arrived from the inhabitants of Bohemia, requesting from the Emperor, and also from the King his brother, the necessary troops and means to pacify that kingdom: this the Emperor granted at a later period.

Before the departure of the Emperor from Wittenberg, certain conditions or offers of reconciliation and *amende honorable* had been proposed by the Electors of Saxony and of Brandenburg, in the name of the Landgrave of Hesse; but the Emperor rejected them, because they were of too general a nature and offered little importance or guarantee.* Another document was then submitted to him, which, after having been approved by the same Electors and by the Landgrave, was examined by the Emperor, who accepted it to content all parties.† The conditions having been ratified by all parties concerned, the Landgrave of Hesse waited upon His Majesty in the town of Halle, where he admitted his error, and did act of obedience as he ought to do.‡ The Emperor

* Per serem musto geraes, e de pouca emportanciá e seguranra.

† E bem visto e considerado de Sua Magestade polos contentar a todos o quis arreitar.

‡ Eseguindo a disposiçaõ delle sendo per todos ratificado, o ditto

ordered his general to keep him guarded, which, according to the stipulations, he ought and had a right to do.* And although then and afterwards the said Landgrave and the Electors have pretended that the Emperor acted wrongly, by giving to the document signed an interpretation conformable to his own wishes,† it cannot, nevertheless, be denied, that the Emperor could not have acted otherwise than he did, and that what he did do was in keeping with the convention.‡

A great number of princes and towns of the North, who had adhered to the Smalcald League, and who had taken part in the said wars, admitting their error, tendered their submission to the Emperor; and the other cities, which had not joined the league, and had not taken part in the wars, sent deputies to to do the due and customary homage and tender submission.§

As is often the case with soldiers who, as soon as they are unemployed, feel the want of doing something, it happened that as the Emperor had no work

Lantsgrave se veo appresentar na ditta cidade de Alla a Sua Majestade onde despois deronhecer sua culpa, e dar a obediencia que devia.

* Que conforme ao ditto papel se devia e podia fazer.

† Interpretando o escritto conformea seus desejos.

‡ Contudo não se pode negar que o Emperador pode fazer o que fez, e que o que fez foi conforme ao papel.

§ Para lhe fazer e dar adevida e costumada obediencia, e reconherimento.

for them,* they mutinied amongst themselves, nation against nation, and differences arose which it was no easy task to settle. Nevertheless, the Emperor regulated all, and established such good order that, having found the time and means to separate them, he assigned them different habitations, so that all differences and all the causes of disturbance vanished. Having done this, the Emperor started for Nüremberg, and, according to the intentions spoken of above, he convoked a Diet at Augsburg.

After these two great victories, which God, in His boundless goodness, designed to grant to the Emperor,† he received from various countries a great number of embassies, and some brought him expressions of congratulation which by no means came from the heart.‡ In fact, the machinations which were then discovered, before and afterwards; the agitation which manifested itself at Naples; the conspiracy of Count Fiesco at Genoa; the isolated movements, caused perhaps by foreign intrigue, which broke out at Sienna, and other events already mentioned, sufficed to indicate the existence

---

* Como he cousa ordinaria entre os soldados, que quando estão ociosos, buscam em que se empregar, não tendo o Emperador cousa em que os occupar.

† Estas duas tão grandes victorias alcançadas, que Deus foi servido por sua immensa condade de dar aoEmperador.

‡ Algūs lhe mandaram dar os parabems, que estavam bem pezarosos.

of a wish and attempt to disturb and prevent the accomplishment of so good a work, and at the same time the prosperity of the Emperor's affairs.*

There were some persons who abstained from taking a greater share in events, despairing of success. But later they were so sorry for it that, in endeavouring to find a remedy, they destroyed what they had done and established, and matters changed to this point that they were obliged to modify their designs and dissimulate their wishes. If those persons are not such as they ought to be, may God remedy it, as He has done for the past, by regulating matters in such guise that their desires shall not be accomplished.†

All this having been done, the Emperor left Nüremberg, where he had an attack of the jaundice. He had almost recovered, when, having continued his journey as far as Augsburg, he had a relapse, and he was so

* Porque pelas pratticas, que naquelle tempo, hum pouco antes e despois, se descobriram, assi da inquietação que ouve em Napoles, como da quella que o conde de Fiesco fez em Genova, e doutras paxoes particulares, que por ventura per instigação d'algûs se moveram entre os de Sena, et outras de que se tem feito menção, se pode bem julgar a tenção e vontade, que havia de perturbar e impedir tão boa obra, e as cousas do Emperador.

† Taes pode ser dexeiram de se metter mais neste negocios, desconfiando do bono successo delles, dos quaes despois o arrependimento foi tal, que querendo remediar, perderam o que tinham feito e posto da sua parte, e as cousas se trocaram de maneira que ellas foram forçados a mudar seus desenhos e dissimular suas vontades. Se ellas não são quaes derem ser, Deus o queira remediar, como fezo passado, ordenando as cousas de maneira, que seus desejos não teveram effeito.

weakened by it that he suffered from it a long time after his arrival. Before he was perfectly convalescent, he made his proposition to the Diet, to take into consideration a remedy for the affairs which were brought before it, and which all tended to the service of God, to the welfare, tranquillity, and union of Germany, and to its defence against whomsoever should dare to attack it.* The Diet had already commenced its sittings when the King of the Romans arrived, who had succeeded in subjecting Bohemia to obedience to him. The Queen dowager of Hungary arrived a little later at the same city of Augsburg, on divers matters upon what she had to settle at this time. After the jaundice, the Emperor had an attack of the gout; and although it was not so general as his previous attacks, he suffered from it at various intervals and divers parts, so that it lasted till the spring of 1548. This was his fourteenth attack; and, in the spring, to hasten his convalescence, he took a concoction of China-wood.†

During the Imperial Diet of Augsburg various hostile machinations were set on foot, tending to prevent the good results alluded to higher up.‡ In

---

* Para que se tratasse do remedio das cousas nella contendas, as quaes todas eram encaminhados ao serviço de Deus, bem, tranquilli dode, e união de Germania, e defensáõ contra os que a quiessem offender.

† Saxifrax (?).

‡ Duruado a ditta dieta imperial, ouve algúas pratticas todas contrarias e para impedir o bem effeito do que arima se trattou.

this same Diet the Emperor succeeded in inducing the
States of the Empire to submit to the Council, which
he had always claimed, as stated previously, ever since
1529.* But at the moment when that council convoked at Trent was called upon to exercise the
highest influence, Pope Paul, by a *motu proprio*,
wished to transfer it to Bologna, and convoke it
himself, God knows with what intentions.† The
Emperor, seeing the great evils that might arise
therefrom, opposed it, and consequently prevented it,
insisting so strongly that the said council remained
at Trent.‡

The Emperor had recovered from the jaundice,
and one day, whilst out hunting with a view to
regain strength, he received certain news from Placentia, which informed him that, in consequence of
the severity of Duke Peter Louis, son of the said
Pope Paul, and the hardships he inflicted upon the
inhabitants, they had risen against him, and having
taken possession of the town, they offered to hand it
over to whomsoever offered them the most favourable

* Tamhem o concilio, que, como ditto he, desde o anno 29 o
Emperador tinha sempre procurado, e tanto feito, que pelos estados
do Imperio na ditta dietta se acceitou.

† No mesmo tempo, quando se havia de dar maior calor, o Papa
Paulo de seu motu proprio tentou de o transferir a Bolonha, e avocar
a si: com que tenção isto fosse, Deus o sabe.

‡ Vendo o Emperador o grande mal, que disto poderia resultar, o
contradisse, e impedio sempre, e de tal modo persistio, que o ditto
concilio esta em Trento.

conditions. The governor of the state of Milan accepted, in the name of His Majesty, the propositions made to him, before anyone could enter the Duchy of Placentia. The Emperor, from the reasons mentioned, and also to preserve and guard the rights of the Empire,* ratified and confirmed that treaty.

Despite all this, and despite the machinations 1548 alluded to above, suitable measures were taken at the Diet of Augsburg, to attain the object of its meeting; and, as regards religion, a regulation was adopted, which was to be observed until the Council at Trent should have pronounced itself.†

At the same time the German soldiers who formed the Emperor's body-guard mutinied. This produced more scandal than danger,‡ as, on investigating the cause of the mutiny, it was found that it was to be attributed to the interests of some isolated individuals rather than to the ill-will of the soldiers.

The Diet adopted all the resolutions that it could,§ and as it had been sitting a long time, the Emperor, on the advice of the King his brother, and of the

---

* Polas causas dittas, e tamben por conserva e guardar o direito do Imperio.

† Não obstante tudo isto e as pratticas dantes dittas, se trattou na ditta dietta o que convinha para o effeito e fim polo qual se ajuntara, e quanto a religião, hum modo de viver atee que o concilio se cele-brasse em Trento.

‡ Que foi causa de maior scandalo que de perigo.

§ E tendo se concluido nella o quo entao se pode concluir

said Estates, addressed to it a good proposition;* the Diet then broke up, and the members returned home.

Before the departure of the King, the Emperor's brother, their Majesties agreed upon the marriage of the eldest daughter of the Emperor with the eldest son of the King his brother, who assumed the title of King of Bohemia; and as the Emperor entertained the intention and the desire to send for his son, the Prince of Spain, that he might visit his States and make the acquaintance of his vassals,† he begged the King his brother, and the King his son-in-law, to proceed to Spain, for the marriage of the said son-in-law, and that he should remain there in the name of Emperor, to govern those kingdoms during the absence of the Prince his son; to which they consented. Thus the said King of Bohemia left Augsburg, and passing through Italy, embarked at Genoa, landed at Barcelona, and from thence posted to Valladolid, where the nuptials were celebrated. The King of the Romans also left shortly afterwards to look after his interests; the Emperor remained a few days longer to complete what still remained to be done.

After arranging all his affairs, the Emperor took his departure from Augsburg, after leaving two thousand Spanish troops in garrison in three strong-

* Húa boa prattica.
† Para ver aquelles terras e ser conherido de seus vassallos.

holds of Würtemberg, and after having withdrawn the troops which had been sent to Augsburg. Having thus provided for the welfare and good order of public affairs,* he took the road to Ulm, from which city he also withdrew the garrison, taking a portion of it with him. He then took the direction of Spires, by the Rhine to Cologne. This was the ninth time that he made this journey, and the eighth time he visited the Netherlands.

The Emperor found the Queen his sister at Louvain, from which city he proceeded to Brussels, to look after his own affairs as well as to attend to those of his States of the Netherlands.

---

* Deixando a republica bem provida e ordenada.

LONDON
PRINTED BY SPOTTISWOODE AND CO.
NEW-STREET SQUARE

M

Printed in the United States
83746LV00004B/72/A